Facing Life's Problems
Help from the Book of Nehemiah

MARTHA L. TYLER

Regular Baptist Press
1300 North Meacham Road
Schaumburg, Illinois 60173-4806

FACING LIFE'S PROBLEMS: HELP FROM THE BOOK OF NEHEMIAH
© 1997
Regular Baptist Press
Schaumburg, Illinois

Printed in U.S.A.
All rights reserved

Contents

Preface	....	5
Introduction	....	7
Lesson 1	Our Greatest Resource	11
Lesson 2	Nothing Is Impossible with God	19
Lesson 3	How to Do a Great Work for God	27
Lesson 4	How to Treat Those Who Wrong You	36
Lesson 5	What to Do When Everything Goes Wrong ..	44
Lesson 6	Money: A Test of Your Spiritual Character ..	52
Lesson 7	Back to the Bible	61
Lesson 8	Why Is the House of God Forsaken?	69
Lesson 9	Freedom from Fear	77
Lesson 10	Problems! Problems! Problems!	85
Lesson 11	Rekindling Your Spiritual Passion	93
Lesson 12	Lessons from Nehemiah	101
Leader's Guide	....	111

Dedication

To my husband, Don, who is a
constant source of encouragement to me;
and to Callie Butler, who assisted me
in typing the manuscript for this book.

Preface

MAYBE YOU are thinking, "The book of Nehemiah? A Bible study for *women*?" Yes, it certainly can be! And I trust that before you finish this study, the man Nehemiah will become your new friend as you journey with him through trials and triumphs.

I also hope these lessons will cause the book of Nehemiah to come alive for you. Nehemiah faced problems that are common to you and me. He referred to "the God of Heaven" as the help for his problems. This same God is waiting to help us if only we will turn to Him.

It is my desire for these lessons to (1) help you know the facts about the book of Nehemiah; (2) teach you how to handle life's problems by following Nehemiah's example; and (3) stir a desire within you to apply these lessons to your daily life.

Each lesson is divided into three parts: The first part of the lesson (before the questions) is a condensed overview of the subject or Scriptures being studied. The second part, the questions, is designed to help you think about the subject. Many of the questions are simple to answer, but I hope they will help you understand the Biblical truths. And third, "Make It Personal" and "Put It into Practice" are to help you apply the truths you learned.

The first eight lessons go through the book of Nehemiah. The next three are on topics found in the book: fear, handling problems, and renewing our spiritual fire. The last lesson is a review of the previous eleven.

May these lessons be a help and encouragement to your Christian life.

Suggestions for Individual Study
1. Before you begin each study, pray that God will help you understand it and apply it to your life.
2. Read the entire book of Nehemiah. (Do this at one setting if possible.) It is only thirteen chapters.
3. Use a reliable modern translation of the Bible alongside the King James Version. (A parallel Bible has two translations side by side. If you have one, use it.)
4. Look up any unfamiliar words, names, or places in a Bible dictionary, if you have one.
5. Read the lesson and write your answers in the space provided before your group study.
6. Think about the questions at the beginning of the lesson in preparation for your study.
7. Use "Put It into Practice" at the end of the lesson to apply some of the truths that God impressed upon you in the lesson.

Suggestions for Group Study
1. Follow the suggestions for individual study and come to the group study prepared.
2. Be willing to take part in discussion. Be open, but also be careful not to say things that would embarrass your family or friends. Share things God has taught you in your individual study.
3. Stick to the passage being studied—don't get sidetracked.
4. Listen to what others say. You may be surprised at their insights. Commend them for sharing their thoughts—this will encourage some of the more hesitant members to participate in discussion.

Introduction

LET'S LOOK at the background of the book of Nehemiah.

Who wrote the book?
According to Nehemiah 1:1, it was written by Nehemiah, the son of Hachaliah.

Who was this man Nehemiah?
The only time he is mentioned in the Bible is in the book of Nehemiah. He was a plain, ordinary person like you and me, yet he was highly motivated to do a difficult job for God. He rose from obscurity to national prominence. He was probably born in slavery, yet he made his way to one of the top-level positions in the Persian Empire, one of the grandest empires in history. Many would have reveled in his position, but his heart was elsewhere—in Jerusalem.

Nehemiah was a fantastic organizer and pragmatic leader. He had great power in prayer and knew God was his final resource in any success. He did not act without prayer and did not pray without acting.

When was the book written?
During the reign of Artaxerxes (465–424 B.C.).

What is the background of this book?
The Jewish nation started with Abraham and his descendants: Isaac, Jacob, and Joseph. The people multiplied greatly while serving as slaves in Egypt. Eventually Moses led the Israelites out of Egypt to the threshold of Canaan, their Promised Land. Under Joshua the people entered and conquered the land. For several hundred years the only leadership was provided by various judges whom God raised up to lead His people.

When the people demanded a king, God allowed them to choose Saul. His reign was marked by disobedience, and God raised up a new king, David. Following the reign of David, which was marked by great military success, his son Solomon reigned until his death.

At that time Solomon's son Rehoboam became king; however, he disregarded the counsel of Solomon's advisors, and the nation was divided. Ten tribes formed the Northern Kingdom of Israel; two tribes formed the Southern Kingdom of Judah.

The Northern Kingdom never had a good king. The people were captured by the Assyrians in 722 B.C. A few people escaped to the Southern Kingdom, but the rest were never heard of again.

The Southern Kingdom, Judah, lasted until 586 B.C. Nebuchadnezzar conquered Jerusalem and took many of the Jews to Babylon as slaves (2 Kings 25:1-8, 11, 18-21). The soldiers burned the temple and carried many of the beautiful items from the temple back to Babylon (2 Kings 25:13-17; 2 Chronicles 36:18). Most of the other buildings in the city were destroyed, along with the city wall (2 Kings 25:9, 10).

God did not forget His people. Eventually the Persians overthrew the Babylonians, and God used King Cyrus to accomplish His ultimate plan. After the Jews had been in captivity for seventy years, Cyrus allowed the first group of Jews to return to Jerusalem to rebuild the temple under the leadership of Zerubbabel (2 Chronicles 36:20-23; Ezra 1:1-4; 5:2). Eighty years later, Ezra led back another group. When Cyrus died, Artaxerxes (pronounced Are-taz-erk-sees) became king, and Nehemiah was his cupbearer. Thirteen years after Ezra's return, Nehemiah led a group back to Jerusalem to build the city wall.

Why was it important to build the wall?

City walls kept a city safe from bands of robbers. In the case of the Jews in Jerusalem, the walls would also help to keep the people from being assimilated by the pagan nations around them. The Jews had started to intermarry with the Gentiles and were beginning to lose their distinctive culture, language, and religion. Nehemiah did not want this trend to continue.

What is the key verse?

"Then answered I them, and said unto them, the God of heaven, he will prosper us; therefore we his servants will arise and build: but ye have no portion, nor right, nor memorial, in Jerusalem" (Nehemiah 2:20).

What questions should you ask as you study this book?

1. What does the passage mean in its historic, Biblical context?

2. What practical lessons can I apply to my life today?

LESSON 1

Our Greatest Resource
Nehemiah 1

NEHEMIAH faced many crises in his life, but he found the most powerful way to handle them—he prayed.

Nehemiah was not a king or great celebrity. Actually, he was a slave who rose to a prominent place in ancient Middle Eastern politics and business. He was just an ordinary person like you and me.

T... ... t Nehemiah's background, ... Hachaliah (Nehemiah 1:1) ... hemiah lived in the Persi... ... rt was in Jerusalem. And ... ew the background mater... ... appened to Jerusalem.)

O... ... rusalem's devastation, a... ... (Nehemiah 1:1–4). But h... ... alem when he was only a ... s like an impossible proble... ... difficult problems. The G... ... blem can help you and me...

Ne... ... the walls around Jerusal... ... Christian life. The practic... ... ...iah are timeless, reliable guidelines that will work today if we apply them. The

11

book uncovers practices to follow and problems to avoid. These same principles can help us build our lives for God. This lesson, "Our Greatest Resource," teaches us how prayer can be the resource for life's problems.

Questions to ask yourself: What concerns are on my heart right now? Am I facing some impossible situations? Is a problem breaking my heart?

❊ ❊ ❊

1. When Nehemiah heard of the conditions in Jerusalem, his heart broke, but he knew the right resource for his problems. What four things did he do, according to Nehemiah 1:4?

Nehemiah knew the Jews' plight had resulted from sin against God (Nehemiah 1:4–7). On one hand, he believed God's promises; on the other hand, he knew God was tired of His people's lack of obedience. (God's judgment for sin had sent the Jews into exile [2 Chronicles 36:13–17].)

Nehemiah didn't just feel bad because of the conditions of God's holy city; he *mourned* over Jerusalem—and he expressed his grief to the point of physically weeping.

What do you do when your heart is broken? Have you ever faced a situation that looked impossible? Did you try to work it out yourself, or did you turn to God?

2. When we ask God to help us, it is important to begin with confession of sin. Why is confession important, according to Psalm 66:18?

3. Many years after the psalms were written, 1 John 1:9 was written. As you read it, notice that it sheds more light on the confession of sin. In the original language, the word "confess" is in the present tense, meaning "to continually confess sin." Confessing our sins should be as natural to us as breathing. We should develop a habit of continually

confessing our sins. How can we do this?

4. Nehemiah had a right view of God. In Nehemiah 1:5 how did Nehemiah describe God and show his reverence and respect for Him?

Whom did Nehemiah serve on earth? The king. How did King Artaxerxes compare to God? There was no comparison! Nehemiah put things in right perspective. Even though King Artaxerxes was the greatest king on earth at that time, God was greater. Remember, even though your problems seem great, God is greater.

5. Compare Jeremiah 17:5 with Jeremiah 17:7. What is the difference between a person God curses and one whom He blesses?
Curses:

Blesses:

Which one are you like most of the time?

6. Read Nehemiah 1:6 and 7. Notice that Nehemiah used the personal pronouns "I" and "we." He took responsibility for his part of the sin. Sometimes we have a tendency to blame others for our sins. Whom did Nehemiah say had sinned?

7. The marvelous thing about confessing sin is that the result (being forgiven) is contagious. When we see how God forgives us, what should we do for others? Read Ephesians 4:32.

8. (a) Read Psalm 51:3. What did the psalmist say about his sins as he confessed them?

(b) Whom did he say he had sinned against (v. 4)?

9. We need a fresh realization that sin is against God. Sin is not some little mistake that can be overlooked. When Potiphar's wife tried to entice Joseph to commit adultery, how did Joseph view this sin (Genesis 39:9)?

Sin is disobeying God's Word. After we have realized our sin and confessed it, we need to claim God's promises to help us not commit that sin again. (See John 15:7; Romans 8:28-32; Philippians 4:13; Jude 24.)

Read Nehemiah 1:8 and 9. Nehemiah was actually claiming what God had promised in Leviticus 26 (especially verses 40-46). God had said He would bless His people for obeying His Word and punish them if they did not. An important part of prayer is claiming the promises of God. Since Nehemiah would later plan to build the wall of Jerusalem, these particular promises of Israel's restoration were meaningful to him.

10. What does Hebrews 4:16 tell us to do?

Nehemiah believed that prayer would transform God's promises into reality. God wants us to believe Him, to claim His promises, and to trust Him for answered prayer. Prayer is not overcoming God's reluctance, but claiming God's willingness.

11. What is the first word of Nehemiah 1:8?

Sometimes we are not good at remembering. Have you ever forgotten something you promised a child, only to have that child remind you? God never forgets His promises. He wants us to have faith in Him.

George Mueller founded and directed a large orphanage in England. He determined to ask no one for money for the orphanage and to depend completely upon God to supply his needs. One day someone asked Mueller to suggest some verses for strengthening one's faith. Some of those verses are listed below.

12. How can these verses strengthen your faith?
    John 14:13, 14

    Hebrews 11:6

    1 John 5:14, 15

    Jeremiah 33:3

13. In Joshua 4:20–24 we read that the Israelites set up stones to remind them of how God had helped them cross the Jordan River. What are some ways you can remind yourself of God's past blessings?

14. For what two things did Nehemiah ask God in Nehemiah 1:11?

Nehemiah practiced what some people call model-and-serial-number prayer. Did you ever need a new part for an appliance? You needed to specify the model and serial number to get the right part. Likewise, we need to be specific in our prayers to God. Have you ever experienced an answer to this kind of praying? Could you share it?

15. Read Luke 11:5–10. (a) What specific request did the man make (v. 5)?

(b) Why was his request granted (v. 8)?

(c) According to verses 9 and 10, what is the lesson for us?

Often our vague praying is a result of our unbelief. Would you ask someone to "come over and have dinner sometime," or would you ask, "Could you have dinner with us at 7:00 this Friday night?" You would be specific. We need to be specific in our praying too.

It should encourage us that God answered Nehemiah's prayer. (The king granted his request.) It all started because one person cared about God's work, confessed sin, and claimed God's promises. It was not easy, but the results were worth the effort it took. Are you willing to take the necessary steps to answered prayer?

❃ ❃ ❃

Make It Personal

Prayer develops some important qualities in our lives. First, it develops patience. Prayer teaches us to wait on God (Psalms 25:5; 123:2). Our first response to a problem should be prayer. Have you ever started putting something together and found that you could not figure out how to do it? Then you read the instructions and learned how it really went together. Sometimes we rush into projects, confront difficulties—then we pray! How much better to wait on God first. Too often we are like the two men out on the ocean in a lifeboat. After they had used all of their provisions, one man turned to the other and said, "I guess we had better pray about this." The other man replied, "Has it come to that?"

Second, prayer teaches us a proper view of life. Have you ever looked down at the ground from an airplane? How much different the view is from the sky than from on the ground! God sees the end from the beginning, not just one tiny section of our lives. When we try to view things from His perspective, our thinking changes and our view of life becomes more like His.

Third, prayer gives us a sense of peace. In this world of turmoil and chaos, prayer brings peace to our hearts (Philippians 4:6, 7).

Finally, prayer makes us more successful. Nehemiah prayed 120 days before he started the project. ("Chisleu" in Nehemiah 1:1 is December; "Nisan" in Nehemiah 2:1 is April.) He built the walls in only 52 days (without all the modern equipment we have today). Nehemiah prayed twice as long as he worked. He prayed for four months so he could get the job done in two months (Nehemiah 6:15). Often our failures are due to lack of prayer.

How can each of the following things improve your prayer life?

A time to pray

A plan to pray with written requests

A journal of answered prayer

Difficult situations in life

Take a minute to think about the personal questions at the beginning of this lesson (p. 12). Why not follow Nehemiah's example to help you solve these problems?

I believe it is important to have a time each day for prayer and Bible study, but it is also important to have an attitude of prayer all day long. (Read 1 Thessalonians 5:17.)

Several years ago my husband and I started putting our most important concerns on a 3" x 5" card and praying together for them each day. We have seen some wonderful answers to prayer.

❄ ❄ ❄

Put It into Practice
(For personal challenge, not class discussion.)

Most people want a great prayer life, but often they are unwilling to pay the price to have one. Here are some suggestions that could help you develop your prayer life.

1. Set a time and take time for prayer each day.
2. Have a specific place to pray.
3. Find a prayer promise to claim.
4. Make a list of concerns for which to pray.
5. Find a prayer partner to pray with you (Matthew 18:19, 20). Your spouse or a close friend would be a good partner.

Which of these suggestions can you put into practice right away?

The great old hymn "What a Friend We Have in Jesus" says it well:

>*"O what peace we often forfeit,*
>*O what needless pain we bear,*
>*All because we do not carry*
>*Everything to God in prayer!"*

LESSON 2

Nothing Is Impossible with God
Nehemiah 2: 1–9

HOW DO YOU handle the challenges of life? by praying? by taking action? Which should you do? Often we give up and don't do either one.

Nehemiah, however, did both. His life shows a balance between dependency on God and action on his own part. Both are taught in Scripture. John 15:5 says, "Without me ye can do nothing"; James 1:22 states, "But be ye doers of the word, and not hearers only, deceiving your own selves." Nehemiah combined both principles, and he showed careful planning in carrying them out.

Although he was a slave, Nehemiah held a coveted—but quite dangerous—position. He was the king's cupbearer, and as such he would taste the king's food and drink before serving it. If the food were poisoned, the lowly cupbearer would find out first. The position was dangerous for another reason: the cupbearer had to be happy and cheerful around the king, because being sad in the king's presence was a crime worthy of death. Despite the dangers of the job, the position was coveted; the king and his cupbearer often became very close friends. A cupbearer could be extremely influential in his king's decision-making process.

It was while Nehemiah was a cupbearer that he learned of

the need in Jerusalem. He wanted to help, but he was far away from Jerusalem and had no rights and no money. He realized his only resource for help was God.

Do you have any seemingly impossible problems? Are you struggling with a marriage that seems to have unsolvable problems? Do you have a wayward or disrespectful child or a difficult parent or in-law? God specializes in hard cases. His Word reassures us, "The things which are impossible with men are possible with God" (Luke 18:27).

What did Nehemiah do? He prayed (Nehemiah 1:5-11). He also realized that the only man who could help was King Artaxerxes. However, the king had earlier ordered the work in Jerusalem to stop. Artaxerxes was a Persian, and Persian rulers did not change their minds. Even today people refer to "the law of the Medes and Persians" when they want to emphasize stubbornness or a refusal to compromise.

What a predicament! Nehemiah needed the king's goodwill to remedy the problem, and only God could turn Artaxerxes' heart toward him. Nehemiah believed that God would intercede, so he started planning how to build the walls of Jerusalem. He figured out what would be needed. Then every day he waited to see how God would answer his prayer. Four long months passed. Then it happened!

While the king and queen reclined after eating a sumptuous meal served by Nehemiah, Artaxerxes noticed Nehemiah's changed facial expression and asked why he looked sad (Nehemiah 2:1, 2). Nehemiah knew he was in a precarious situation (v. 2). He tactfully presented his cause to the king (v. 3). Surprisingly the king asked, "Can I help?" Nehemiah prayed quickly (v. 4). Because he had done his homework, he knew exactly what he needed and told the king (vv. 5-8). Nehemiah had the unique balance of faith and realism.

What a challenge to us today! We need to bring our problems to God, depend upon Him to work them out and still be realistic enough to think through our problems, allowing God to direct us.

Questions to ask yourself: What do I need to trust God for in my life today? Am I trusting Him? Am I allowing Him to guide me to practical solutions?

1. Nehemiah had a well-thought-through plan; he knew exactly what he needed. For what did he ask in Nehemiah 2:5, 7, and 8?

2. What is the relationship to the king's question in Nehemiah 2:2 and Nehemiah's prayer in 1:11?

Our prayers tell a lot about us. Can you think of some things you pray about every day? Those are the things that truly concern you. Someone has said that our prayer habits are the key to our successes and failures. When will we ever learn that it pays to pray?

3. Nehemiah's prayer was the key to his success. How was Nehemiah's prayer answered? See Nehemiah 2:8.

When Nehemiah heard of the conditions in Jerusalem (Nehemiah 1:3), he had to make a choice. He could have said he felt pity for the people in Jerusalem and left it at that. Or he could have charged off to see the king and used some high-powered salesmanship on him. He did neither! He waited on God to guide him.

4. How do you respond when you hear bad news about your friends and loved ones? Nehemiah chose to turn to God in prayer. How did the truths found in Proverbs 21:1 influence Nehemiah's thinking and action?

Prayer helped Nehemiah make the right choice. He, like Moses, chose to suffer with God's people rather than enjoy the pleasures of the palace (Hebrews 11:25, 26). Nehemiah chose to leave the luxury of the palace to live under primitive conditions in the ruins of Jerusalem.

5. How does Nehemiah's example help us in making right choices in our lives?

Life's choices fix our character. Often the choices we face are not between good and bad, but between better and best. To some degree, we are a product of the choices we have made in life. God did not make us robots; He gave us the ability to make choices.

6. Read Nehemiah 1:5 and 11. Nehemiah had a knowledge of God. What conclusions can we draw from Nehemiah's view of God?

7. What do the following verses reveal concerning God's power?
Jeremiah 32:17, 27

Luke 1:37; 18:27

8. How can the verses you just read encourage you regarding your problems?

Nothing Is Impossible with God 23

9. The king saw a change in Nehemiah's countenance (Nehemiah 2:2). What, according to Proverbs 15:13 and 15, is the connection between a person's heart and her countenance?

Nehemiah had prayed and planned and had apparently hidden his feelings from the king for four months. However, everyone has a breaking point. Nehemiah had reached his, and his face showed it.

10. (a) When the king noticed Nehemiah's sad countenance, how did Nehemiah respond emotionally (Nehemiah 2:2)?

(b) How does Proverbs 20:2 relate to Nehemiah's position?

Sometimes we like to think that Bible characters always reacted perfectly. Nehemiah was afraid, just as you and I would have been—and rightly so. Nehemiah's life was at stake. He had prayed for God's blessing and favor; then he faced possible execution. Nehemiah's antidote for fear was to turn to God for help.

11. In Psalm 31:13 the psalmist faced fear and terror all around him. His life was threatened. According to verses 14 and 16, how did he respond?

Nehemiah responded the same way.

12. Previous prayer and planning enabled Nehemiah to be honest with the king and to tell him his problem. How did the king respond? See Nehemiah 2:4.

Nehemiah had prayed and fasted for four months. When the crisis came, he just breathed a quick prayer to God for help.

13. How does God promise to help us in times of trouble? Read Psalms 50:15 and 91:15.

14. Nehemiah was in trouble. According to Ezra 4:17–22, what had Artaxerxes commanded years earlier?

Nehemiah was basically asking the king to change his mind, and King Artaxerxes was famous for *not* changing his mind.

It is obvious that Nehemiah lived in a spirit of prayer. A spirit of prayer should characterize our lives too (1 Thessalonians 5:17). We should pray about big problems and small problems. We should pray about the ordinary things of life. We should pray when we are driving the car or when we are talking to someone—during the daily routines of life.

Bible commentators have speculated about why Nehemiah mentioned the queen (2:6). Perhaps it was because women, by nature, tend to have softer hearts. Artaxerxes was known as a king who followed the laws of the land and made no exceptions. Maybe Nehemiah felt the queen was more approachable than her husband. Perhaps Nehemiah had good rapport with the queen and felt she would be on his side. Anyway, it is unique that the writer mentioned the queen.

15. (a) What two questions did the king asked in Nehemiah 2:6?

(b) How do these questions indicate that the king was happy with Nehemiah's work?

By spending four months in prayer, Nehemiah knew what to tell the king. His answer was to the point; he did not ramble. By faith, he had planned what he would need to complete the task of rebuilding the walls. He was aware of the problems he would face.

• He needed safe passage through different provinces.

• He needed proper credentials to present to those who hated the Jews and would try to stop his work.

• He needed building materials.

Wisely he did not mention the king's previous decision to halt the work in Jerusalem (Ezra 4:21).

16. How can Nehemiah's example of praying, planning, and boldness help us take risks and action for God?

Make It Personal

Not all oranges that come from Florida are good. Some trees actually grow sour oranges. These trees cannot produce sweet oranges unless they are grafted to a sweet orange tree. In our natural state, we are like the sour orange trees. We cannot produce spiritual fruit. We need to have a new nature grafted into us. This happens when we accept Jesus Christ as our Savior (Romans 7:4-6; 2 Corinthians 5:17). Once we have made that decision, we can come to God with the confidence that He will hear and answer our prayers (1 John 5:13-15). We can trust Him to do impossible things for us.

We need God's help in order to have effective prayer lives. We need to pray as the disciples did, "Lord, teach us to pray" (Luke 11:1).

1. What did the psalmist write about prayer in Psalm 116:1 and 2?

2. How do these verses characterize Nehemiah's life?

3. How can these verses apply to our lives?

How did you answer the questions at the beginning of the lesson (pp. 20, 21)? What do you need to trust God for in your life today? this week?

Put It into Practice
(For personal challenge, not class discussion.)

1. What action can you pursue this week to put this lesson into practice?

2. How can you make that action a habit in your life?

LESSON 3

How to Do a Great Work for God
Nehemiah 2; 3

NEHEMIAH certainly did a great work for God, and he is a good example for us if we want to do a great work for God. Nehemiah rebuilt the wall around Jerusalem in fifty-two days, despite opposition—especially from Sanballat and Tobiah. How did he do it?

He was a master planner. He planned how to build the wall and what materials he would need even before he received the king's permission to build. After he arrived in Jerusalem, Nehemiah took steps to execute his commission. He went out at night and, with his own eyes, determined the condition of the wall (Nehemiah 2:13–15). Then he finalized a plan for restoring it. His ultimate success was phenomenal.

Nehemiah was a master at motivation. He took a group of discouraged Jews who were living in ruins (Nehemiah 1:3) and motivated them to "rise up and build." Nehemiah did a great work for God and led others to do so too.

Nehemiah followed some important principles in completing his new assignment. To do a great work for God, we, too, must be able to influence people rightly. Perhaps you are a Sunday School teacher, a children's church worker, or a mom who is trying to raise godly children. These principles should help you with the role God has given you.

28 FACING LIFE'S PROBLEMS

Questions to ask yourself: Why do I think most Christians fail in leading others to "do a great work for God"? What great work am I attempting for God? Am I doing it in my own strength or in God's strength?

How to Influence and Lead Others
1. (a) To influence people we must value them. Why were people valuable to Nehemiah's work?

   (b) Why are people valuable to us?

All Christians have the responsibility of influencing others to accept Christ. We are told that at least 90 percent of all people who receive Christ as their Savior say they were influenced to do so by a friend or family member.

Who are you influencing for God?

2. If you would volunteer to tell how a friend or family member encouraged you to accept Christ as Savior, write your testimony here. Did that person consider you valuable? Of course!

3. Doing a work for God is never without opposition. Name the enemies of God's work who are mentioned in Nehemiah

2:10. (You will see their names again later in the book.)

4. If we are to lead and influence others, we must place a high value on them. Notice in chapter 3 that Nehemiah acknowledged *by name* the people who worked on the wall, where they worked, and what they did. What does this acknowledgment indicate about Nehemiah's feelings for them?

5. We need to be doing right ourselves before we can influence or lead others. Nehemiah was honest and open about why he had come to Jerusalem; even his enemies knew. What was his reason? See Nehemiah 2:10.

6. Nehemiah was a great motivator. What did he say to rally the people to want to build the wall? See Nehemiah 2:17 and 18.

Nehemiah set a goal high enough to stretch the people, but at the same time, he gave them confidence that God would help them overcome the obstacles.

Assumptions That Will Help Develop and Motivate Others

An assumption is an opinion that something is true. First, we should consider two *wrong* assumptions:

Wrong assumption #1: *People are not interested.*

Nehemiah did not assume that, since the people had not had a wall for years, they did not want a wall, or that they were happy with the status quo. Such an assumption would have been incorrect.

30 FACING LIFE'S PROBLEMS

Wrong assumption #2: *I have nothing to offer.*

Nehemiah could have concluded, "I don't know a thing about building a wall. I'm used to life in the king's palace. I can't help these people." Such an assumption would have been wrong.

7. Regardless of how inadequate you feel, if God calls you to a task, He will enable you. Nehemiah led a feeble group of people to do a great task for God. What promise does God give us in 1 Thessalonians 5:24?

Here are three *right* assumptions:

Right Assumption #1: *People want to feel important and worthwhile.*

We need to help people develop their self-respect. (This is good to do for our family members too.) Make them feel important and useful. Help them find satisfaction from their usefulness.

8. List some things we can do to help others feel important.

Right Assumption #2: *People respond to encouragement better than to criticism.*

9. Christians should encourage one another. (a) According to 1 Corinthians 16:17 and 18, how did Stephanas, Fortunatus, and Achaicus encourage Paul?

(b) In return, how did Paul think those men should be encouraged for their efforts (v. 18)?

Canada geese fly in a V formation—and for a good reason: the lead goose splits the wind resistance, making flying easier for the rest of the flock. The lead goose flaps hard, but the other geese merely cruise along. When the lead goose gets tired, it falls back into the V formation, and another goose takes the lead. In that way, the geese help each other.

Chickens are totally different. Have you ever seen an injured chicken in a pen with other chickens? All the rest start pecking at it. If they are uninterrupted, they will peck the injured chicken until it dies.

Have you ever seen people act like chickens? Do you treat people like the goose or the chicken? Do you help others or peck at them?

10. (a) In the following verses, which fowl do the people represent? Why?
Nehemiah 2:17, 20

Nehemiah 2:10, 19

(b) What can you do to encourage other Christians?

Right Assumption #3: *People need to believe in us before they are willing to follow our plans and ideas.*

People do not buy into what we *do* but what we *are*. Nehemiah laid the whole case before the Jews. He challenged them to build and told them the good news of God's hand on him. The people perceived that Nehemiah was in Jerusalem for their good.

11. According to Nehemiah 2:12, what had Nehemiah not told anyone in Jerusalem?

Later (vv. 17, 18) Nehemiah gathered the people together; at that time he was ready to talk to them.

The Jews believed that God had put into Nehemiah's heart the plan to rebuild the wall. They believed in Nehemiah as a person, and they were, therefore, willing to follow his plans and ideas.

12. Nehemiah was able to influence people from all walks of life to help build the walls. Who were the first people mentioned (Nehemiah 3:1)?

The priests led the way, followed by gatekeepers, guards, goldsmiths, common people, and, yes, even women (Nehemiah 3:12). Those young women were not afraid to do hard work. They joined their father to do a great work for God.

13. Underline in your Bible the three words in Nehemiah 3:10, 23, 28, 29, and 30 that indicate that people worked on the portion of the wall that was close to their own houses.

Nehemiah tried to have the people build near their homes or where they had an interest. Why? Doing God's work in our homes and places of interest appeals powerfully to our hearts. We know and understand best the people and places closest to us. Doing a good work near our homes is important in Christian service. No amount of Christian work elsewhere will compensate for neglect of our families.

In using our influence rightly for God, we need to ask ourselves some questions: Why am I doing this project? Am I selfishly trying to build my dream and use people, or will this job be for the mutual advantage of others and me?

14. What is the difference between manipulation and motivation?

People eventually see through manipulation.

15. Why was the building of the wall for the good of the Jews?

To be properly motivated, people need to know what is expected of them. Notice how Nehemiah accomplished this goal. He divided the volunteer work force into many parts. Each group had a specific task—some cleared away stones, some picked out usable stones, some were stone masons, others were superintendents of the work. Each one knew what was expected of him.

16. Why is knowing what is expected of you important?

Nehemiah placed people where they could do their best work. Some had to build the wall from scratch (Nehemiah 3:2), while others had to repair a broken-down section (v. 4). The people were united and zealous, and each one was willing to do the work assigned to him.

17. Where on the wall did the priests do repair work (Nehemiah 3:1)?

Nehemiah placed a high priority on the job the people did. He showed this priority by recording the names of thirty-eight people who worked on the wall, and in thirty cases, he even added the name of the person's father.

18. What common phrase is used for Malchijah and Hashub (3:11), Ezer (v. 19), Baruch (v. 20), Meremoth (v. 21), and Hananiah (v. 30)?

Nehemiah recognized those who did extra work.

34 FACING LIFE'S PROBLEMS

19. (a) Some people will not cooperate with us or help us reach our goals. Who refused to cooperate with Nehemiah (Nehemiah 3:5)?

(b) Apparently Nehemiah did not take time to straighten out the troublemakers. He just kept building. What can we learn from Nehemiah on how we should react to the troublemakers in our lives?

(c) What would have happened if Nehemiah had directed his time and energy to getting the nobles to do the work he wanted them to do?

❦ ❦ ❦
Make It Personal

Here are some ways we can give support and assistance to the people we are trying to influence and lead:

1. We must genuinely love and care for each person. People don't care how much we know until they know how much we care.

2. We need to maximize people's strengths and minimize their weaknesses.

3. We need to spend time with the people we lead. We can *attract* people at a distance but *impact* them only up close.

4. We need to give them ownership of their work. People support what they help create.

5. We need to help people succeed in their jobs—make our expectations clear.

6. We need to eliminate unnecessary burdens that hinder people from succeeding in their jobs.

7. We need to catch people doing something good and praise them for it. In a recent survey, most people admitted they could do their secular jobs better if they wanted to do so. Surely this is true in church work too.

What work for God do you have to do? Read the previous seven points again and think of ways you can apply them to your work for God.

If those around you are not reaching their potential, look at yourself. Could you change and be a greater help to them? Nehemiah set a good example of helping people reach their potential.

❈ ❈ ❈

Put It into Practice
(For personal challenge, not class discussion.)

1. Which of the principles in this lesson could help you impact the lives of others?

2. Reword the above answer into a prayer.

3. How does God want you to respond to this lesson?

4. Earlier in the lesson you wrote the name of a person or persons you are influencing for God. What steps can you take to better influence that person (or persons), as well as others, this week?

LESSON 4

How to Treat Those Who Wrong You
Nehemiah 4:1-10

HAVE PEOPLE ever mocked you or made fun of you? Everyone of us has experienced ridicule at some point in her life. Ridicule indicates that we are doing something. There is a saying, "If a wagon is moving, it will kick up some dust." Likewise, if a Christian is doing something for God, she will "kick up dust," she will suffer ridicule. Second Timothy 3:12 says, "Yea, and all that will live godly in Christ Jesus shall suffer persecution." Being ridiculed for doing right is an indication of a godly life.

As we continue our study in the practical book of Nehemiah on how to face problems, we will consider what to do when people misunderstand us and make fun of us.

Unfair ridicule is a tool of the Devil to discourage believers. No one wants to have people laugh at her. The Devil uses this tool to keep unbelievers from accepting Christ too. Some people hesitate to accept Jesus as Savior because they are afraid that others will make fun of them.

Nehemiah faced ridicule. Nehemiah 2:19 tells us, "They [Sanballat, Tobiah, and Geshem] laughed us to scorn, and despised us." Nehemiah knew how it felt to be made fun of. (See Nehemiah 4:1-3.)

Questions to ask yourself: What am I doing in life that will count for eternity? Have I ever been criticized for doing that?

❈ ❈ ❈

Let's look at how Nehemiah handled ridicule, as recorded in Nehemiah 4.

1. (a) According to Nehemiah 4:1, how did Sanballat react when he heard that the Jews were building the walls?

   (b) What negative thing did he first say about the Jews (4:2)?

Some people today consider God's people a feeble minority. Some honestly believe this world would be better off without Christians to hinder them. The world measures things by what they see, such as how big or affluent or powerful something may be. Therefore, Christian causes do not impress them.

2. What did Sanballat imply about the Jews' work (4:2)?

You have probably seen pictures of cities that have been destroyed by war. If you can recall such a picture, you have a good idea of the way Jerusalem looked in Nehemiah's day. It was a hopeless-looking mess. God is in the business of taking an irreparable mess and making something beautiful out of it. This happens every time we see a hopeless, helpless sinner accept Christ as Savior and become a new creature in Christ (2 Corinthians 5:17).

Sanballat mocked the foolishness of the Jews' faith, but the Jews believed God wanted them to build the wall and that He would help them do so.

Many unbelievers consider living the Christian life a waste of time; they also believe that Christians waste their money by tithing and giving generously to the church. Have you ever had someone think that it was ridiculous for you to give money to the church—especially if you give a lot?

3. Noah is an example of a man who probably was ridiculed for his faith, since no one but his family accepted his message. Based on Hebrews 11:7 and Genesis 6:13—7:16, what choices did he make?

God blessed Noah and spared him and his family in the Flood. Are you making choices that show you have faith? Nehemiah kept looking through "eyes of faith" even though he was criticized by those around him.

4. (a) What did Tobiah say about the wall (Nehemiah 4:3)?

   (b) What did his comparison imply?

5. Unsaved people often do not understand our Christian work and life. Their eyes are focused only on earthly interests. What they don't realize is that the only actions that will last are the ones done for God. What does 1 John 2:17 say about this subject?

6. The values of Christians and the values of this world should be different. Read Luke 12:16-21.
   (a) What mistake did the rich man in this parable make?

   (b) What values should he have had (v. 21)?

What do you really value? Where are you laying up treasure?

7. Nehemiah reacted to ridicule quite interestingly. He considered the source. What three people are identified as the source of ridicule in Nehemiah 2:19?

   (a)

   (b)

   (c)

Nehemiah realized that those men were troublemakers. He identified them for what they really were. Always consider the character of the people who laugh at you. Christ warned us that not all people will speak well of us. (We are known not only by our friends, but also by our enemies.) In this world we can expect opposition (John 16:33). We should handle criticism in the spirit and attitude in which it is given—we should consider the source.

8. What do our friends and enemies reveal about our character?

9. What kind of opposition did Nehemiah face, according to Nehemiah 4:7 and 8?

Why do ungodly people ridicule believers? One reason is jealousy. At other times it's because they are convicted of their own need. Often ungodly people substitute laughter (or ridicule) for logic.

10. (a) Our Lord faced ridicule. How did people treat Christ, according to Mark 5:40?

(b) How was Christ treated on the cross? Read Luke 23:35 and 36.

The believer is in good company when he is criticized unjustly. The servant is not greater than his master.

11. Nehemiah considered the compensation he would receive from doing right before God. As stated in Matthew 5:11, we are blessed when people do what three things against us?
    (a)

    (b)

    (c)

12. Why should we be happy about this, according to Matthew 5:12?

13. Read 1 Peter 3:14–17 and answer the following questions. Be prepared to discuss how the answers can relate to you today.
    (a) We are blessed, or happy, for doing what (v. 14)?

    (b) What are we to do in our hearts (v. 15)?

    (c) What are we to be prepared to do (v. 15)?

    (d) How are we to do it (v. 15)?

(e) What are some practical ways of giving an answer concerning our faith in Christ to other people?

(f) What will make the one who ridicules you ashamed (v. 16)?

Nehemiah was a good example of handling ridicule in a godly way. He kept on doing God's work without getting angry or sidetracked.

14. (a) According to 1 Peter 3:17, is it better to suffer for doing good or evil?

(b) Why?

Nehemiah 6:15 tells us that Nehemiah and the Jews finished the wall in just fifty-two days. Unbelievable!

15. How did the enemy react when the wall was finished (Nehemiah 6:16)?

There comes a time when the scoffer will be silenced. Even though Christ was ridiculed and treated shamefully when He was here on earth, a day is coming when it will be different.

16. How does Philippians 2:9–11 describe this coming time?

Here are some facts to consider when you face ridicule. First, consider who is doing the laughing and ridiculing. Ask yourself, "Why are they laughing?" Look around to see if they are laughing at others. If so, why? Consider what is going to happen to those who ridicule others.

17. What advice does Proverbs 24:29 give us?

The Jews did not quit because of ridicule. Their theme was "Praise God and pass the bricks." But the enemy didn't quit either.

18. According to Nehemiah 4:6, why did the work keep going forward?

19. What attitude should we have toward those who ridicule us? Read 1 Peter 3:8 and 9.

Someone has observed that few people live the Christian life consistently all their lives. Nehemiah is an example of the exception to that trend. He stayed at the intended task and built the walls (Nehemiah 6:15).

Nehemiah reacted to derision with determination. He reacted to ridicule with resolution. When the walls were finished, the enemy stopped laughing. You never know what you can do until you try it. William Carey, a great missionary of the past, said, "Expect great things from God, Attempt great things for God."

Make It Personal

We all face times in our lives when people do not treat us right. Sometimes persecution or ridicule comes from the world around us; at other times it comes from our own brothers and sisters in Christ. Looking at the source of the criticism and trying to understand the motive for it helps us not to take it quite so personally. Learning to take our hurts to God and letting Him work out the problems is an indication of spiritual growth.

Here are seven principles from Romans 12:14–21 that can help us when we are mistreated.

1. Say something good about the strengths of our enemies (v. 14).

2. Promote harmony with humility. All hostility flows out of pride (v. 16). (Have you noticed that most family fights evolve out of pride?)

3. Refuse retaliation (v. 17). Christians often retaliate by verbal blows.

4. Remember our testimony (v. 17). Our lives need to be open and honest before the world around us.

5. Try to get along with others if we possibly can (v. 18). We must do our part before God regardless of the other person's response.

6. Do not seek revenge (v. 19).

7. Let "good" be our weapon to overcome evil (v. 21).

Try to apply these seven principles to a situation where someone has wronged you. Experience how God will lift your burden and give you peace.

Put It into Practice
(For personal challenge, not class discussion.)

1. Don't let your critics demoralize you. Take courage in the Lord (Psalm 27). He gives us the victory.

2. Which one of the principles in this lesson will help you handle criticism better?

3. Reword that principle into a prayer.

4. Review the personal questions at the beginning of this lesson. What are you doing that will live on even after you are dead? Have you ever received criticism or ridicule for doing it? Could you handle the criticism better now?

LESSON 5

What to Do When Everything Goes Wrong
Nehemiah 4:10–23

EVERYONE has discouragement in her life at some time or another. Christian women are not exempt. Isn't it amazing how complicated life can become? All Nehemiah planned to do was build a wall around Jerusalem—a rather simple project. He should have been able to accomplish his goal in a few weeks and then return to Persia. However, it seems that nothing is as simple as we think. The more Nehemiah tried to alleviate the Jews' problems, the greater they became.

When Sanballat heard that the walls were being built, he became angry and ridiculed the Jews (Nehemiah 4:1). Tobiah stood at his side and sarcastically said that a fox could knock the walls down. This criticism led first to open opposition and then to conspiracy. No matter how hard Nehemiah tried to straighten out the problems, they only grew worse and seemed to multiply.

A mother of three preschoolers saw a mama skunk parade her babies across the backyard just in front of her own toddlers. "Run! Run!" she shouted. Whereupon each child grabbed a skunk and ran into the house.

Have you ever been in a similar situation where bad became

worse? What happened next? Did you become discouraged? Discouragement can take the wind out of our sails. In fact, rare is the person who can handle discouragement well.

Questions to ask yourself: What discourages me? How do I handle discouraging situations? Have I ever given my best effort to do something for God only to feel that my project failed?

Nehemiah faced discouragement as he built the wall. We, too, face discouragement as we build the spiritual walls in our Christian life. To build a strong fortification, we must start with a proper foundation.

1. According to 1 Corinthians 3:11, Christ should be our foundation. What does this mean?

Satan doesn't want us to build our spiritual life. One of his major tools to slow down or stop our building is discouragement.

2. (a) According to Nehemiah 4:10, who became discouraged?

   (b) Why was their strength giving out?

We need to recognize when we have too much to do. We must learn to give up doing good things in order to do the best things. Sometimes we strive to do more than God intended for us to do. Learning to prioritize will go a long way in fending off discouragement.

3. Name some great servants of God in the Bible who fell prey to discouragement due to overwork.

46 FACING LIFE'S PROBLEMS

4. (a) What causes discouragement?

   (b) How do some people react when they become discouraged?

Here are some characteristics of people who easily become discouraged.
- They are supersensitive to criticism.
- They are constantly aware of their weaknesses.
- They have an abnormal amount of pride in their achievements.
- They have unattainable goals and ambition beyond their abilities. They never quite accomplish what they have planned.
- They are jealous and envious of others' success.
- They are greedy and covet things they are unable to attain.

Do any of these characteristics describe you?

5. Nehemiah was at a crucial point. How high had the wall been built (Nehemiah 4:6)?

The halfway point in anything can be discouraging. For instance, many married couples experience hardship at the halfway point of their marriage. Generally, the newly married and the older married get along fine. But the time in between can be dangerous. During middle age people are more likely to suffer what we call "midlife crisis." King David's sin with Bathsheba happened in his middle age. We need to keep our relationship with our mates alive and vibrant not only in middle age but in every age.

6. What are some ways to build a good marriage?

7. The Jews were discouraged. What were their enemies threatening to do (Nehemiah 4:11)?

The Jews were worn out from wading around in broken stones and burned timbers. Their enemies were threatening them. All the rubbish around them made their job look insurmountable. Their fatigue was both physical and emotional.

8. How does Proverbs 24:10 apply to their situation?

Rubbish was the source of their burden. What burdens are you carrying? Is there some rubbish in your life that contributes to your burdens? We cannot build our lives on trash. Some years ago a developer built an entire housing subdivision on a trash dump. In a few years the foundations shifted, the walls cracked, and the whole subdivision went to ruin.

9. How should we build, according to Proverbs 24:3 and 4?

The enemies were attacking the Jews mentally. They kept saying, "We're going to get you!" The Jews started believing what their enemies were saying; they started thinking negatively. Similarly, much of our Christian warfare is fought mentally.

10. What does Philippians 4:8 tell us to think about?

We can endure a difficult crisis if we retain strong convictions. Here is a conviction we should develop: We are here for a purpose, with a cause to pursue, with a Person to love, and with a goal to achieve for God. But some people have "stinkin' thinkin'." Keep your convictions strong; guard your thinking.

11. What does Proverbs 23:7a tell us about our thinking?

48 FACING LIFE'S PROBLEMS

The Jews reacted to their problems by thinking negatively. How often we see the same reaction in our churches today. Usually we can handle negative talk from the world—we expect it from that source—but when it comes from our own brothers and sisters in Christ, it really discourages us. We need to guard our thinking and try to see the "big picture" the way God does. We need to focus on God and do the King's business. One pastor was asked how many active members he had in his church. He replied, "All are active—some are building up and some are tearing down." Which are you?

12. Proper thinking involves having faith in God. What did Jesus tell His disciples in Mark 11:22-24?

Faith is an antidote for discouragement. Faith in God helps us keep our thinking right. Here are some ways we can guard our thinking:
Watch what we put into our minds. Remember that the computer slogan "Garbage in; garbage out" is true of our minds. We must watch what we see, hear, and read.
Focus on helping others. Discouraged people think too much about themselves.
Develop a sense of self-worth. We are valuable to God.
Don't feel sorry for ourselves. Keep this thought in mind: "This too shall pass."

13. What did Nehemiah do to give hope and encouragement to the discouraged Jewish builders (Nehemiah 4:13, 14)?

We, too, must arm ourselves against discouragement. To do this, we need to develop a proper perspective in the following areas of life:

God. He is in control. He is in control of our birth, our death, and everything in between.

Self. We must not take ourselves too seriously.

Problems. No matter how big our problem, someone else has a bigger one. We will always have problems.

People. People are different from each other, and some are difficult to understand.

Time. We must live life in the light of eternity.

Nehemiah armed himself against discouragement by prayer (Nehemiah 4:4). In addition, he armed himself against discouragement by remembering what the Scripture states about God (4:14), His greatness, and His help in times of trouble.

14. According to Romans 15:4, what is the purpose of the Scriptures?

Discouragement can have a positive as well as a negative effect on our lives. What happens when a great athlete makes a mistake or a great musician messes up his performance? He may feel somewhat discouraged, but he can't wait for the next sporting event or concert or competition, because he knows he can do better.

15. What does Proverbs 24:16 say about a righteous man?

Nothing else reveals our strengths or our weaknesses like discouragement. We must learn to deal with discouragement in a positive way.

Nehemiah motivated the people to be brave (Nehemiah 4:14). We cannot run from our problems. *Life is problems.* Nehemiah stood up and said, "Don't be afraid of the enemy." We are fearful by nature; therefore, we should consciously try *not* to focus on danger. Instead of focusing on our problems, we should look at what we call "the big picture." That is what Nehemiah did. He encouraged the Jews to see the entire situation. He motivated them to action for a great cause.

We need to keep our problems in proper perspective. Sometimes we lose our focus. We forget why we are serving God. We major on our tiny, unimportant problems. We need to remember what really counts, because that view will keep us on course. We need to focus on our eternal priorities.

16. Most women love security, but remember life has no foolproof plans. There are no risk-free arrangements; God is our only security.
    (a) How does Matthew 6:25 emphasize this point?

    (b) How do Matthew 6:32 and 33 emphasize this point?

Nehemiah got the people back to work (Nehemiah 4:15). A great cure for discouragement is to get back to work. We cannot feel our way out of discouragement; we must choose to work our way out of it. So don't say, "I don't feel like doing that job." Just do it! If you feel overwhelmed by the magnitude of the job, do what you can do today. Then do that each day. Most importantly, look to God to help you be big enough for the job!

The people spread out across the wall, building close to their homes or places of interest. While they built, each worker carried a weapon.

17. (a) According to Nehemiah 4:19 and 20, what plan did Nehemiah have to fight should the enemy appear?

    (b) Nehemiah 4:20 records the reason the people could have confidence in battle. What was the reason?

(c) To Whom should we look to fight our battles?

❦ ❦ ❦
Make It Personal
Christians need to get rid of rubbish that hinders their service for God and promotes discouragement. They need to get back to the "wall" of Christian service in their lives.

What can we do? We can begin by not insisting on having our "rights"! We can't always have everything that is coming to us. If we insist on always getting what is rightfully ours, we will become *resentful*—because someone else got what we should have had; *bitter*—because life is *not* fair; *angry*—because things do not go as we would like; *hateful*—because we are frustrated; *fearful*—because of lack of trust in God.

Some things are worth fighting for, and some are not. Things usually work out best when we allow the Lord to fight our battles for us.

❦ ❦ ❦
Put It into Practice
(For personal challenge, not class discussion.)

How can you handle discouragement?

1. Make sure you know Jesus Christ as your personal Savior.
2. Confess known sins in your life.
3. Determine to practice Philippians 4:8; refuse to think negatively.
4. Develop strong spiritual convictions (Ephesians 4:14).
5. Claim appropriate Scriptures for discouraging situations. (Psalm 42:11 and Jeremiah 29:11 have encouraged my heart many times.)
6. Get busy for God. Don't sit around feeling sorry for yourself.
7. Seek ways to encourage your family and friends this week. This will help melt away discouragement.

LESSON 6

Money: A Test of Your Spiritual Character
Nehemiah 5:1–13

NEHEMIAH 5 records a new problem that Nehemiah encountered; it had to do with money. It would do little good to build a wall to keep the enemy out if the people themselves were going to destroy one another by dissension over financial matters.

We, too, face the problem of money. In some way or another, each of us struggles with materialism. Television commercials and magazine advertising convince us that we *need* it all, and credit card companies promise that we can *have* it all. Poor people ask, "Why don't I have enough?" Rich people ponder, "How much is enough?" Older people wonder, "Will I have enough to last my lifetime?"

As women we have a lot of influence on how much money our families will spend on food, clothing, housing, vacations, and even automobiles. Someone said, "A woman can throw more out the back door than a man can bring in the front door." Because we have such influence, we need to have right attitudes toward finances. A financially informed woman can influence her family in making wise purchases and saving for the future.

Money: A Test of Your Spiritual Character 53

Questions to ask yourself: What is it about money that causes divisions? Is money a source of conflict in my home? Do I constantly keep wanting more and more? Have I embraced this world's materialistic view of life?

Money and the Jews

The Jews were having grave financial problems, such as starvation, slavery, gigantic debt, and enormous taxes (Nehemiah 5). These problems were creating division among the people, and for good reason.

1. What problem is recorded in each of these verses?
   (a) Nehemiah 5:1 and 2

   (b) Nehemiah 5:3

   (c) Nehemiah 5:4

Because of overpopulation, a recent famine, and high taxation, food was scarce. The mothers were crying out, too, because their children had been sold into slavery (v. 5). Others had mortgaged their fields, vineyards, and houses and were in the process of losing them. Taxes were the source of others' poverty because Judea, like other Persian provinces, had to pay tribute.

Financial pressures can be extremely stressful. One quip summarizes what happens in some marriages: "He is fast on the deposit, but she is quicker on the draw." Churches have financial problems too. Often the problem is not a lack of money but a lack of wisdom and consensus on how to spend the money.

2. How did Nehemiah react when he heard of the problem (Nehemiah 5:6)?

54   FACING LIFE'S PROBLEMS

3. (a) What were the greedy rich people doing wrong (Nehemiah 5:7)?

   (b) What had God commanded in Exodus 22:25 and Leviticus 25:35–37?

   (c) How did God instruct the Israelites to handle a situation like the one in Nehemiah's day (Leviticus 25:35)?

   (d) According to Leviticus 25:37 and 39, what three things were they *not* to do in such a situation?

God often uses money to show the strengths and weaknesses of our character. Our actions toward money are an outward expression of our inward spirituality. How we handle money is a good indicator of our trust in God.

4. Nehemiah set a great example of not taking financial advantage of the people.
   (a) What did he *not* do that other governors had done (Nehemiah 5:14, 15, 17, 18)?

   (b) What else did he *not* do (Nehemiah 5:16)?

   (c) Why did Nehemiah do right (Nehemiah 5:15)?

Money and Me

Before we condemn the greedy Jews in chapter 5 too much, let's look at our attitude toward material things. Let's ask ourselves nine heart-searching questions that will monitor our view of money.

Do I love to give to God?

5. (a) Where did Jesus urge His disciples *not* to "store up treasures" (Matthew 6:19)?

   (b) Where did Jesus urge His disciples *to* "store up treasures" (v. 20)?

   (c) Why should we store treasures in Heaven (v. 20)?

   (d) Read 2 Corinthians 9:6–10. What are the two ways to sow?

People may hesitate to give generously to God's work for fear they will not have enough left to meet their needs, but God says the person who gives little will receive little. Don't let a lack of faith rob you of God's blessing.

   (e) According to 2 Corinthians 9:7, what attitude should we *not* have in giving?

   (f) In 2 Corinthians 9:8 what promise does God give to believers who give generously?

God gives us resources to use and invest for Him. As we give to God, He gives back to us. When we invest what God has given us in His work, He will provide us with even more to give.

56 FACING LIFE'S PROBLEMS

Am I generous to others? God blesses generosity and judges stinginess. As we give to others, we receive (Ecclesiastes 11:1). There is joy in giving that brightens our day, makes our burden lighter, and gives us indescribable pleasure.

6. (a) What principles about giving do we find in the following verses?
   Proverbs 11:24

   Proverbs 11:25

   Proverbs 11:26

   (b) What does Luke 6:38 teach about giving to God?

   (c) List three material things that make you happy.

True happiness does not come from material things; it comes from a right relationship with God and others.

   (d) Put a check mark next to the things that money cannot buy:

   ____ appetite   ____ house
   ____ bed   ____ knowledge
   ____ books   ____ loving companionship
   ____ eternal life   ____ medicine
   ____ food   ____ peace
   ____ friends   ____ pleasures of life
   ____ good home life   ____ purpose to live
   ____ happiness   ____ sleep
   ____ health   ____ the good life

Material things never satisfy our significant needs. Real wealth is everything money cannot buy and death cannot take away.

Am I jealous and envious of others? Do we look at what others have and feel that we should have it too? Do we think that we "owe" it to ourselves?

Jealousy and envy often rob us of lessons God wants to teach us. Perhaps God wants to teach us to trust Him. He may want to teach us that we can get along without all the toys and trinkets our friends have.

Jealousy takes many forms. What happens when one of our fellow believers has great success in his career? He may not find rejoicing and acceptance among other Christians. Someone has said that when a person makes his mark in the world, a lot of people start showing up with erasers.

The backlash of this jealousy spills over even to something as simple as buying a new dress, for instance. When complimented on it, we don't want to cause anyone to envy us, so we say, "Oh, it was on sale. I hardly paid anything for it."

7. Read Psalm 49:16 and 17. Why should we not be jealous of others' material blessings?

Am I preoccupied with "things"? Are we living more for the present world than the one to come? How are we spending our time?

8. (a) In 1 Timothy 6:17 and 18 what warning does God give to those who have been materially successful?

   (b) Why is it wrong to put too great an emphasis on material things? Read Proverbs 23:4 and 5.

Money is a wonderful servant but a terrible master. Do not confuse temporal benefits with eternal benefits.

Have material things taken away my desire to serve God? Sometimes we don't realize this has happened to us.

9. What principle do we find concerning this danger in Matthew 6:24?

Am I grateful for what God has given me?

10. (a) How do we accumulate our possessions? Read Deuteronomy 8:18.

   (b) How should we react when we consider all God has done for us? Read Psalm 92:1 and 2.

Am I willing to work? Do you think the world (or the government or somebody else) owes you a living? God places value on work.

11. (a) How does 2 Thessalonians 3:10 emphasize this fact?

God blesses work (Titus 3:14), but He condemns dishonesty and laziness. Laziness often accompanies high living. It usually starts with the misuse of credit, which encourages overspending and impulse buying. This results in a never-ending stream of charge slips that cannot be paid. Marital tension rises. Depression may accompany this situation. Often the people in this predicament go around telling others what a tough time they are having in hopes that sympathy will bring comfort. The bottom line is that they are lazy, overindulgent, and irresponsible, and they insist on a standard of living that they simply cannot afford.

(b) What object lesson is given in Proverbs 24:30–34?

Do I place my hope and value in possessions?

12. (a) Read Proverbs 11:28. Why is hoping in and valuing possessions wrong?

(b) In light of Psalm 49:10, why is it important not to make material things the focus of our lives?

Materialism is an issue of our priorities more than of our possessions. It is our attitude toward possessions that counts.

Do I constantly want more? It is possible to have little but to be quite materialistic and to constantly want more.

13. What warning do 1 Timothy 6:9 and 10 give us?

Luke 12:15 states, "A man's life consisteth not in the abundance of the things which he possesseth."

Make It Personal

Both Christians and non-Christians struggle with materialism. The Christian woman may or may not have financially more than those around her, but that is not what distinguishes her from the non-Christian. What makes her different is her attitude toward material things. Her treasure is not on earth but in Heaven (Matthew 6:19–21). For the Christian woman, money is a great resource with which she can serve others (1 Timothy 6:18).

If someone were to write a biography of your life, an important document to use for research would be your checkbook. Your checkbook reveals your values in life (Matthew 6:21). Would yours reflect giving to God's work and wise financial management? One test of your Christian character is how you use money.

Before we were married, my husband and I decided to give more than a tithe to God. Don was still in college after we married, and we did not make much money, but we still gave to God what we had purposed in our hearts. God provided our needs, and we were able to pay all our bills (including college tuition). We truly experienced Malachi 3:10.

❀ ❀ ❀

Put It into Practice
(For personal challenge, not class discussion.)

1. Determine to honor God by giving at least 10 percent of your income to His work.

2. Study your income and expenses. If you have not already done so, draw up a workable budget. Don't make it so detailed that it is impossible to follow. Periodically review your budget to see if you are still on target.

3. Examine your attitude toward material things. Do they have too great a hold on your life? Remember you cannot serve God and money. Try to think of some actions you can take to change your attitude—actions such as trusting God to supply your needs, looking for ways you can help others, and praying for wisdom in financial decisions.

LESSON 7

Back to the Bible
Nehemiah 8:1–18

A HUSHED CROWD watched as Ezra and thirteen of his helpers ascended a newly built wooden platform. The people had asked Ezra to expound the Scriptures to them. They stood "from morning until midday" while Ezra read. What had led to that occasion?

God had directed His people to rebuild His city. Thirteen years earlier, Ezra, a scribe and priest, had led a group of Jews from Babylon to Jerusalem to reestablish worship in the recently *rebuilt temple.* Then under Nehemiah they *rebuilt the walls.* On the day that Ezra read the Scriptures, the Jews began to *rebuild their spiritual lives,* not with stones and mortar, but with the Word of God. They had gathered to hear Ezra read from a simple scroll. The powerful words he read invoked a response that changed their lives. The people praised God, felt deep conviction of sin, changed their behavior, and pledged to serve Him. This is the kind of revival we need today.

The people of Israel lived under foreign domination for many more years, but that occasion marked the beginning of some definite changes. They no longer viewed their temple as their guarantee to God's presence or the walls as a guarantee of security. This lesson tells us how the Jews turned to God's Word and shows us the need we have to do likewise.

Questions to ask yourself: What does the Bible mean to me? Do I read it daily? Do I try to make its truths the principles that guide my daily life?

62 FACING LIFE'S PROBLEMS

❈ ❈ ❈

Amazingly the Jews had constructed the walls in fifty-two days. They had accomplished a great deal; they had nice homes, good jobs, and protection from their enemies; but something was missing. The people were hungry to hear God's Word. They had a spiritual vacuum in their lives. They started seeking to fill that vacuum by turning to the correct source.

1. According to Nehemiah 8:1–3, what did they do?

2. Reading and understanding the Bible is the beginning of a godly life. Read Psalm 19:7–11. What does this passage say the Scriptures do for us?
   (a) The law of the Lord (v. 7)—

   (b) The testimony of the Lord (v. 7)—

   (c) The statutes of the Lord (v. 8)—

   (d) The commandments of the Lord (v. 8)—

   (e) The judgments of the Lord (v. 9)—

3. What two things is the Word of God compared to in Psalm 19:10?

The Jews in Nehemiah's day did not have their own personal copies of the Scriptures. How many Bibles do you have in your house? How often do you read your Bible?

4. (a) What did Ezra read on the first day of the seventh month, the Feast of Trumpets (Nehemiah 8:1–3)?

   (b) How long did he read (v. 3)?

   (c) How did the people listen (v. 3)?

   (d) What does it mean to listen attentively?

   (e) How can we listen attentively to God's Word when we hear it taught today?

5. (a) How did the people respond to the reading of God's Word (vv. 5, 6)?

   (b) What did this response reveal about their feelings toward God?

   (c) How do praise and worship go together?

6. What was the Levites' job, according to Nehemiah 8:7 and 8?

Most of the people had been raised in captivity. Hebrew was neither their culture nor their language. They were listening to the Hebrew Scriptures through Babylonian ears; consequently, they needed to have God's Word, the Law, explained to them. It is important that we make the Scriptures clear to those whom we teach formally and for those whom we teach by example.

7. What are some ways we can make the Scriptures clear to our children and friends?

8. Why did the people weep (Nehemiah 8:9)?

How do you feel about sin? Does it upset you when you realize you have sinned? Too often we do not take sin seriously. The Jews had spent a full day absorbed in hearing God's Word. They came to realize that their forefathers' sin had caused them to go into captivity in Babylon. The law commanded them to let the land rest one year out of every seven. They had disobeyed that law for 490 years; therefore, God had caused them to spend 70 years in captivity—one year for each year they had not let the land rest. After hearing Ezra and the Levites read the Law, the people repented of their sins.

Like the Jews, who learned what the Scriptures say and then obeyed them, we need a knowledge of the Bible so we can obey it. True repentance involves being sorry for sin. When was the last time you saw someone cry over her sins? Have you ever cried over yours?

9. Repentance includes being sorry for sin and turning from it. Conviction over sin breaks our hearts. We do not want to continue in the way we have been going. When David repented of his great sin, what did God not despise (Psalm 51:17)?

10. There is another side of repentance over sin; it is the joy of forgiveness. Nehemiah told the people to feast on food and give to those who did not have any. What are the last words in Nehemiah 8:10?

11. There is strength in the joy of the Lord, and Christians should be joyful people. What two things did Jesus say about joy in John 15:11?

Sometimes people think the Bible is sober and sad, but that evaluation is not true. Serving God can be happy and joyful.

On the second day of the month, the people learned that the Law commanded them to hold an eight-day celebration. The Feast of Tabernacles was the last feast commanded in the Levitical law. According to Leviticus 23:33–36, it was to begin five days after the Day of Atonement and last for eight days. Its purpose was to recall the wanderings in the wilderness and the entrance into the Promised Land.

Have you ever been extremely upset and sad about a situation only to find out that God was bringing good from the situation and that you should be celebrating not crying?

12. Read Nehemiah 8:16–18.
    (a) How did the people obey what they had heard from the Scripture (v. 16)?

    (b) How long had it been since the nation of Israel had celebrated the Feast of Tabernacles (v. 17)?

    (c) What did the people do during the Feast of Tabernacles (v. 18)?

What does the Word of God mean to you? How often do you read it? Do you think about it as you go through your daily life? Do you seek to apply it to life's problems and struggles?

13. (a) According to Deuteronomy 6:6–9, what were the Jews to do with God's Word?

(b) How can we apply these verses to our lives today?

Make It Personal

Here are three things we need to do to get "Back to the Bible."

Read It

1. The Bible is true and is our authority for life and practice. Second Timothy 3:16 tells us that the Bible is inspired by God. For what is it profitable?

No other book can you read over and over and still find new truths for your life. I think it is important to read the Bible daily and to have a plan for daily reading (not just open it and read anywhere).

2. What Bible reading plan works well for you?

Back to the Bible 67

My husband and I read a chapter of Proverbs every day. We read the chapter that corresponds to the day of the month. A person can read the book of Psalms in five months by reading a psalm a day. By reading three chapters a day and five on Sunday, a person can read through the entire Bible in one year.

Obey It

3. (a) What does James 1:22 tell us *not* to do?

   (b) What are we to do?

Memorize It

4. Why did the psalmist memorize the Word of God (Psalm 119:11)?

5. We need not only to memorize the Word of God, but according to Psalm 119:15, what else do we need to do?

You can use your devotional time to memorize Scripture and to meditate on it. Review is important in order to retain what you memorize. Some good times to review are just before you go to sleep at night, when you first wake up in the morning, when you are driving alone in the car, when you are put on hold on the telephone, or when you need to wait someplace (e.g., the line in the grocery store, at a long traffic light, in the doctor's office). Can you think of some other times?

Put It into Practice
(For personal challenge, not class discussion.)

Reading the Bible and understanding it is important, but incorporating what we learn from the Bible into our lives is what helps us grow spiritually.

Find a verse or a passage of Scripture that God's Spirit has brought to your attention. Here are some suggestions for incorporating the passage into your life:

1. Summarize what the verse tells you about God.
2. Think about each word of the verse. Think about its overall message.
3. Open your heart to let God speak to you through the passage.
4. As you apply the verse to your life, ask yourself what changes you need to make.
5. Write a response, indicating how you are going to apply this truth to your life.
6. Look for ways you can share this truth with someone else.

LESSON 8

Why Is the House of God Forsaken?
Nehemiah 13

"WHY IS the house of God forsaken?" It was a good question in Nehemiah's day, and it is a good question today. Why don't most people attend church regularly? Do you know Christians who attended your church a year ago but who seldom come today? Do you know others who seem to love God and are active in church but whose children appear to have little spiritual interest and seldom attend church? It is a sad fact that some who are reading this lesson today with spiritual interest will, in years to come, fall by the wayside in spiritual neglect and forsake God's house. Like Nehemiah, we ask, "Why?" Nehemiah 13 gives a number of contributing factors to this problem.

When Nehemiah returned to Babylon (Nehemiah 13:6), he left Eliashib in charge, but Eliashib did not follow in Nehemiah's ways. Nehemiah was surprised to learn how quickly the people had returned to their old ungodly ways. How easily we can do the same thing!

Eliashib gave Tobiah, God's enemy, a splendid apartment in the temple. Previously those rooms had been used to store grain, oil, and wine for the Levites. Disgusted with Eliashib's management, the people withheld their tithe; therefore, the Levites had to return to their farms for their livelihood.

When Nehemiah returned to Jerusalem (Nehemiah 13:7), he

restored the temple services and recalled the Levites to their duties. Then he did some housecleaning. First, he threw out all of Tobiah's possessions; next he purified the rooms and returned them to their former usage.

The people started bringing their tithes to the temple again, because they perceived that the tithes would no longer be misused. Nehemiah reestablished the services in the temple.

Nehemiah also saw merchants selling on the Sabbath. He reminded them of how God had punished their ancestors for that very thing. How easily we forget! The merchants refused to leave, so Nehemiah ordered them out of Jerusalem and stationed guards at the gates to enforce the law.

The people had disobeyed God through intermarriage. (See Exodus 34:14-16 and Deuteronomy 7:1-4.) Their children could not speak Hebrew, which hindered their understanding the Hebrew Scriptures. No wonder the house of God had been forsaken!

Questions to ask yourself: Is faithfulness in church attendance important to me? Do I set a good example of faithful church attendance before my family and friends? Do I support the church by giving regularly to it?

1. The families had failed. They had disobeyed God. To keep the solidarity of the Jewish race, they were to marry Jews only. What had they done, and why was it a problem? Read Nehemiah 13:23 and 24.

2. (a) It is important to teach our children to marry a Christian who loves and serves God. How do 2 Corinthians 6:14 and 15 emphasize this truth?

   (b) How does the world try to influence our children differently?

Why Is the House of God Forsaken? 71

Our families are important to God. We must seek to have godly families. A young pastor once asked an older, well-respected pastor, "Which is the most important—your family or God's work?" The older pastor wisely responded, "My son, your family *is* God's work."

You may be wondering, "What can I do if my children are grown and not living for God?" Blaming yourself or God will not help the situation. You cannot undo the past no matter how much you wish differently. So, what can you do? You can show genuine love, even if your child has greatly embarrassed you. Let him know over and over again that you love him. (You do not love his sin, but you do love him; your child is precious to you.) As long as you have breath and life in your body, pray that God will change your child. Trust God; He is your only hope!

Attending church regularly is an important discipline to build into your family life. Regular exposure to the teaching and preaching of God's Word helps build a strong family.

3. According to Luke 11:28, we are blessed when we do what two things?

Listening alone is not enough. The real purpose of listening to God's Word is to put it into practice (obey it) in our daily lives and become more like Christ. He encourages us to hear and obey His Word.

4. How does our initial faith in Christ begin (Romans 10:17)?

Not only does the Bible message help us begin our Christian life, but it also is the master plan for our day-to-day living.

5. What instruction did Paul give to his young friend Timothy in 1 Timothy 4:13?

It is true that we can and should worship God in our homes, but we cannot separate the worship of God from the hearing of

His Word. We are to discipline ourselves to go and hear the Word of God and then to obey it.

6. (a) We are not only to hear God's Word, but also to honor His day. The Jews had not been honoring God's day. What were the Jews doing on the Sabbath (Nehemiah 13:15, 16)?

   (b) What had they promised to do (Nehemiah 10:31)?

The Sabbath was a day of rest. It was not Sunday, but Saturday (from sunset Friday to sunset Saturday). God rested on the seventh day of creation. He commanded the Jews to do likewise. Observing the Sabbath had always been a hindrance to the Jews' free trade with heathen nations. As a result, some Jewish merchants started putting material gain before their commitment to God.

7. How do people today put material gain before honoring the Lord's Day?

8. What was one of the purposes of the Sabbath (Ezekiel 20:12, 20)?

9. What consequences would Israel suffer if the people did not keep the Sabbath (Jeremiah 17:27)?

10. What consequences may we face if we put material gain before God's commands?

11. According to Nehemiah 13:20, what did the merchants who were trying to sell things on the Sabbath do?

Evil does not leave us easily. Evil in our personal lives leads us first to spiritual laxity and then to doctrinal indifference. We no longer turn to God for our provisions. We lose our spiritual sensitivity and commitment to Him.

When the Pilgrims crossed the Atlantic Ocean in the tiny *Mayflower,* they observed the Lord's Day each Sunday. They reached the new world on a Sunday. However—even though they had spent weeks in their small ship—they waited until Monday to get off the boat and step onto land.

Our nation's view of Sunday has changed greatly since those days. Someone has observed, "Our great-grandfather called it the Holy Sabbath; our grandfather called it the Sabbath; our father called it Sunday; today we call it 'the weekend' (and it is getting weaker all the time)."

12. Because the people in Judah were unfaithful in giving, what had happened to the Levites (Nehemiah 13:10)?

13. After Nehemiah returned to Babylon (Nehemiah 13:6), Malachi, who lived in Jerusalem, exhorted the people. What did he tell them to do (Malachi 3:7–12)?

The people had lost confidence in the priesthood and had started caring for their personal matters; hence they abandoned God's house.

74 FACING LIFE'S PROBLEMS

14. How does 1 Corinthians 16:2 connect giving and regular church attendance?

15. If Christians gave to God as they should, how would the Lord's work be affected?

16. If you have a plan of regular giving to God's work, can you relate how God has blessed you for giving to Him?

Had the Levites trusted God to meet their needs and stayed in Jerusalem, they could have continued to serve the Lord as they had for generations. When David was king, there were so many priests that they all could not serve at the same time, so David divided them into groups. Some were singers; some were gatekeepers; some served inside the temple; and some served outside the temple. No matter what his job, each priest was a part of the whole ministry that glorified God.

This is true of the church today. Each believer is important to contribute to the whole church. Each believer is gifted (see Romans 12:6; 1 Corinthians 12:7; Ephesians 4:7). How has God gifted you? What are you doing for Him? Could you manage your time better and do more for God?

17. As long as Nehemiah was the governor, Eliashib did right. But as soon as Nehemiah left, Eliashib allowed one of his family to marry into Tobiah's family. The word "allied" indicates this relationship (Nehemiah 13:4). Then as a goodwill token, what did he do for Tobiah (v. 5)?

Eliashib believed that the Jews had followed God's law long enough. With an expanding economy, it was the time to "make a deal" with the enemy. Even though Nehemiah was gone, Eliashib still had a critic who lived there and preached against his evil practices. That man was Malachi.

18. What did Malachi say about disobedient practices (Malachi 2:1, 2)?

Unconfessed sin and unholy alliances with the enemy will, in time, deaden spiritual concern and draw the believer away from the house of God. It has been said that few people run well to the end. Don't take back from God in older years what you have given to Him in younger years.

19. As Nehemiah ended his book, what might make you think he was careful to live for the Lord and depend on Him all his life? See Nehemiah 13:22.

Make It Personal

1. How do parents influence their children's attitude about going to church?

2. How can we prepare ourselves *physically* for going to church? How can we prepare ourselves *spiritually*?

3. What kind of influence does your church attendance have on your neighbors?

A deaf boy in Chicago attended D. L. Moody's church. In those days the church had no interpreters for the deaf, and someone asked the boy why he went to church. "To show Whose side I'm on," he replied.

It is important to go to a Bible-teaching church. At times you may get more out of the sermon than at other times, but your attendance is a testimony to the unsaved around you.

If you were to grade yourself on your church attendance, what grade would you give yourself?

Put It into Practice
(For personal challenge, not class discussion.)

A "New Testament" church is one patterned after the churches in the New Testament, according to doctrine, mission, purpose, government, and the like. Why do we need to attend a good New Testament church? Basically to obey the Biblical command (Hebrews 10:25) and to follow the Biblical pattern (Acts 2:42, 46). A key feature of a New Testament church is the preaching of the Word of God. It is from the Bible that we learn about God, Heaven, and Hell. We learn that we have broken God's law and deserve Hell. We also learn that Christ willingly died on the cross and took our punishment for sin. The Bible teaches us how to live pleasing to God and how to lead a joyful, fulfilling life. We need to attend church faithfully. If we go only when we feel like it, we will miss hearing what God wants us to know.

1. Improve your church attendance, if necessary.
2. Seek new ways to get more meaning out of sermons, such as taking notes, telling the message in your own words, and discussing it in a positive light with your family at Sunday dinner.
3. Look for ways to apply the sermon to your everyday life.
4. Invite someone to go to church with you.

LESSON 9

Freedom from Fear

Nehemiah 1—13

WHAT ARE you afraid of? We all have some fears. Charlie Brown claims to handle fear by dreading only *one* day at a time. We can laugh at his sentiment because we all know something about fear. In fact, we live in an age of fear. The best-selling prescription drugs are the ones that help calm our nerves, help us sleep at night, and ease our ulcers—all of which may be fear-related problems.

Fears change as the times in which we live change. Consequently, fears are different today from what they were twenty years ago. A survey among grade school children revealed that twenty years ago children were afraid of animals, dark rooms, and strangers. Today kids are afraid of parents divorcing, school violence, and pollution. What do adults fear? We fear loss of health, wealth, work, friends, and family.

Fear may keep us from reaching our full potential for God. It allows us to function, but not too effectively or happily. It keeps us from being our best for God. We become tentative and make decisions based on what is least frightening or easiest, not on what is right before God. We operate like the father whose son was going to boot camp. He advised his son to be quiet and stay in the middle, which is exactly how many people live. They always try to make decisions that will put them in the middle, where they are least likely to call attention to themselves. Why? Because of fear and unbelief in God's promises.

Questions to ask yourself: What are my greatest fears? How can God help me with them?

1. According to Matthew 13:58, what limited the mighty works of Christ?

2. Read 2 Timothy 1:7. What has God *not* given us, and what *has* He given us?

3. Nehemiah was a man of faith and not of fear. Look at some of the frightening situations Nehemiah faced in chapter 6. Briefly state Nehemiah's circumstances and then write his response of faith.

Fearful Circumstances	**Faith-filled Response**
Nehemiah 6:1, 2, 4	Nehemiah 6:3
Nehemiah 6:5–7	Nehemiah 6:8
Nehemiah 6:10	Nehemiah 6:11, 12

Let's look at some common fears we face.

Confrontation

Most of us do not like to confront people, but at times confrontation becomes necessary. When we confront others, we should do it with a spirit of humility rather than a cantankerous attitude.

    4. How did Nehemiah confront his enemies, as recorded in Nehemiah 13:16–18?

Failure

    5. (a) What do Philippians 3:13 and 14 tell us to do?

       (b) How do these verses apply to our past failures?

    6. Think back over the lessons on Nehemiah. How do you know Nehemiah was not hindered by fear of failure?

Rejection

Nehemiah had to make some highly unpopular decisions. We will probably have to do the same when we follow God. The fear of rejection keeps us from letting God do great works through us. God uses people of faith, not of fear.

    7. (a) What does Proverbs 29:25 say about fear?

(b) What does Proverbs 29:25 say about trust?

Change

Nehemiah changed from a cupbearer to a wall builder to a governor. Be open to let God change you as your circumstances in life change.

8. How can Hebrews 13:8 give us security in a changing world?

Victory over fear

How can we have victory over our fears? We need to discover where fear resides. Fear can come from within or from without. The word "fear" comes from an old English word that means "sudden danger," danger that is real and concrete. This kind of fear helps us escape from physical harm. For example, we teach children not to run into the street because they might be hit by a car. This is fear from without.

But there is a fear within too. It is anxiety-like fear. "Anxiety" comes from a Latin word meaning "feeling tight in the chest." There is no logical reason for this fear. It is caused by "what if" or "might happen" thoughts.

9. Read Philippians 4:6 and 7. What should we do when careful, or anxious, thoughts come into our minds?

10. Read Proverbs 10:24. How does this verse encourage us to release our fears and live for God?

One of the basic needs human beings have is trust, which is the exact opposite of fear. Nehemiah's life exemplified trust in God.

11. List as many incidents as possible that show Nehemiah's trust in God.

A spirit of fear would have kept Nehemiah from doing any of these things. In fact, it probably would have caused him to run away. He obviously did not take all the bad things that were said to him personally, or he would have become so upset that he could not have made rational decisions. The spirit of fear keeps us from being the person God wants us to become.

We can simplify our life by realizing two things: (1) God is in control; and (2) we need to obediently seek God's direction.

12. What does Psalm 37:23 say about God's control?

13. How do Proverbs 3:5 and 6 relate to seeking God's direction?

We all have fears. A little girl asked her daddy if he was afraid of spiders, ghosts, tigers, and all the other things that little girls fear. Amazed that he was not fearful of any of these things, she asked, "Is Mommy the only thing you're afraid of?"

14. According to Psalm 34:4, what did the psalmist do when he was afraid?

Most people fear death. Unless Jesus comes to take us to be with Him, each of us will die someday. We must realize that life is brief.

15. How does James 4:14 describe life?

16. Read Psalm 23:4. Why do we not need to fear death?

Many people try to tiptoe safely to the grave. They are overly cautious; their goal is to die safely. No matter how cautious they are, they are still going to die. Someone has observed that life should come with a warning label that reads, "Life is damaging to your health and will eventually kill you." Realize this fact, and do not let the fear of death immobilize you.

The risk taker and the safety maker will both die. Don't let the spirit of fear keep you from enjoying the life God has given you.

17. Read Psalm 90:12-17. What evidences can you find of the psalmist's realization of the following facts of life?
    (a) Life is brief (v. 12).

    (b) Life should be lived with joy and gladness (v. 14).

    (c) We can make our lives count (v. 17).

Having the right focus is important in realizing freedom from fear. If we want to see fearful situations and problems, we will see them. If we are afraid of failure and see all the possible ways we might fail, we will likely fail. One of my granddaughters, who is afraid of spiders, kept finding the tiniest spiders in our basement. My husband asked, "How does she find these tiny, tiny spiders that we don't notice?" I answered, "She's looking for them, and we are not."

Like my granddaughter, many times we adults find problems and bad situations because we are looking for them. We should, therefore, discipline our minds to think the thoughts God would have us think.

18. Read 2 Corinthians 10:5. What should we do with our thoughts?

We should focus on today more than on yesterday or tomorrow. We build up fear and worry as we think of all the mistakes we made yesterday and the ones we might make tomorrow. Some people lay awake at night counting past mistakes and missed opportunities. If Nehemiah had worried about whether he had handled the problems with Sanballat and Tobiah correctly, he would not have had a clear head and an open heart to let God give him wisdom and guidance to finish the wall.

❉ ❉ ❉

Make It Personal

Don't make the mistake of always living for tomorrow, of dreaming that someday things will be different. We can illustrate life by viewing it as a train trip to a distant station. As we ride along, we envision the wonderful station ahead, with its loving people and unbelievable bliss. It will surely be the ultimate of life. As we ride along, we do not look out the window to enjoy the beautiful scenery, and we do not talk to any fellow passengers. Why? We are focused on our fantasy station.

Maybe you have thought the ultimate (your fantasy station) was to get a good job or to be married. After marriage you thought the ultimate was to have children. Then you thought the ultimate was to have your children leave home. Then you thought the ultimate was retirement. Finally you realize that there is no ultimate in this life. You cannot say, "When I get to _____ stage in life, I will be fulfilled" or "When I get to _____, life will be better." Sooner or later you will realize the truth that "life is in the trip." Whatever we are going to do for God or be for God we must do or be *now*. We cannot just dream that someday will be different. We must not let fear hinder us.

Focus on things you can control. It is impossible to think constructively and destructively at the same time. To get rid of fear, release what you cannot control. What are some things you can and cannot control?

You can control your attitude; you cannot control others' actions.

You can control today's calendar; you cannot control today's circumstances.

You can control your focus; you cannot control life's forecast.

Is the sovereign God controlling your life? Can you trust Him? Yes! Fear increases or decreases in proportion to your trust in God.

❁ ❁ ❁

Put It into Practice
(For personal challenge, not class discussion.)

1. What fears did you list at the beginning of the lesson? Was there a Scripture or a thought in this lesson that could help you with those fears?

2. Reword the above answer into a prayer for God's deliverance from your fear.

3. What action can you take to show that you believe God heard and will answer your prayer?

LESSON 10

Problems! Problems! Problems!
Nehemiah 1—13

PROBLEMS! We all have them. Nehemiah seemed to have more than his share, but with God's help he solved each one as it arose. What a challenge for us!

People react to their problems differently. Some people with insurmountable problems seem to handle them very well. Others are devastated by small problems. We respond to problems by the way we see them: we either run from them, or we approach them. Nehemiah chose to confront his problems. Each time a problem arose, he prayed and just kept on doing the task God had for him.

Question to ask yourself: What problem am I facing now? (You may want to list several.) Take a moment for silent prayer. Ask God to help you understand your problems and how to solve them as you study this lesson.

❖ ❖ ❖

1. Nehemiah had many problems. What were the problems he faced in the following verses? How did he react? Notice how consistent his reaction was as you complete the chart on page 86.

Verses in Nehemiah	Nehemiah's Problem	Nehemiah's Reaction
1:3, 4		
2:1, 2, 4		
4:1-6		
6:1-9		

Often we want a "quick fix" for our problems. We want to solve in ten minutes a problem that took ten years to create. Instead, we should be like Nehemiah, who prayed about his problems and then waited on the Lord for His solutions.

Our past often influences our view of our present problems. How can we use this information to change our reaction to problems? Check one of the following:
- ❏ God does not really understand my problems.
- ❏ God understands my problems, but He might lead me wrongfully.
- ❏ God understands my problems, but I need to know all the details of what I am to do before I follow Him.
- ❏ Because I have seen what God has done in the past, I will trust Him each day to lead me in the future; I will happily be in the center of His will.

Problems! Problems! Problems! 87

Probably everyone knows which one she *should* check; now check the one that is true in your life.

We also view our problems in light of our present surroundings.

2. What were Nehemiah's surroundings like (2:17)?

Nehemiah did not choose a hopeless view of his problems. Instead, he challenged the people to change their thinking.

3. How did he accomplish that change (Nehemiah 2:17, 18)?

We need to focus on God, not on our problems. "Gaze on God and glance at our problems" is a good motto for Christians.

4. What does Colossians 3:2 tell us to do? (The word "affection" means "mind.")

Problems may stop us temporarily, but only we can stop ourselves permanently. Have you ever watched an ant trying to get a crumb of food back to her anthill? What happens when she meets an obstacle? Does she stop?

5. What lessons should we learn from the ant (Proverbs 30:25)?

Even though ants are not strong creatures, they persistently hunt food and store it. Nehemiah was like the ant; each time he faced a problem, he just kept going until he found a way around it.

88 FACING LIFE'S PROBLEMS

Another passage of Scripture that helps us think properly about problems is 1 Peter 5:6–9.

6. (a) What attitude should we have toward ourselves (v. 6)?

(b) What should we do with our problems and why (v. 7)?

(c) What is the Devil's desire for us (v. 8)?

(d) How should we respond to the Devil (vv. 8, 9)?

Problems defeat us when we lack purpose. God wants us to have purpose; it adds zest to our lives. Several adults over the age of one hundred were surveyed to discover what had helped them to live so long. Some had special habits concerning their diet, and others exercised, but the two things they had in common were a purpose to live and a bright outlook on the future.

7. What do the following verses say about longevity?
   (a) Psalm 91:15, 16

   (b) Proverbs 3:1, 2

   (c) Proverbs 9:10, 11

   (d) Exodus 20:12

To handle our problems, we need to develop three outlooks on life.

Desire learning more than leisure

8. We live in a pleasure-crazy age. What do Proverbs 20:13 and 21:17 say about an attitude of always wanting to take it easy and just have fun in life?

Although Nehemiah had one problem after the other, he learned that God was his resource for each one. He seemed to grow stronger after each problem and ready to tackle the next one for God.

All too often we try to avoid the pain of problems. We forget or procrastinate, and some people use alcohol or drugs to deaden themselves, or they "escape" through literature or TV so that they can forget what caused their pain. Often we try to sidestep our problems. Instead, we need to realize that we must learn to handle our problems to grow the way God wants us to grow. Life is not one long vacation.

9. Nehemiah had many problems. What pattern did he always follow when problems arose?

Desire holiness more than happiness

Holiness does not come through a program or a method; it comes from a personal relationship with God. It is the result of an intimate love relationship with our Lord.

10. How did Moses' life demonstrate this principle (Hebrews 11:24, 25)?

90 FACING LIFE'S PROBLEMS

Look for solutions not sympathy
Often we tell our friends our problems, hoping for sympathy in return. Sympathy will make us feel good only for a short while. But Christians have better resources for solutions to their problems.

11. Read Matthew 11:28-30.
    (a) What does Jesus invite *us to do* with our burdens (v. 28)?

    (b) What will Jesus *do for us* if we obey Him and come (v. 28)?

    (c) What two things does Jesus command us to do (v. 29)?

    (d) What is the result of obeying those commands (v. 29)?

When we give God our problems and decide to live for Him, He gives us rest and peace that we cannot attain any other way.

Nehemiah did not go around with a "poor me" attitude. He did not try to find people who would listen to his problem and say, "You poor thing; you are having such a tough time. I can't believe Sanballat and Tobiah are treating you so badly." He did not make mountains out of molehills.

12. Instead of sympathy, what was Nehemiah's solution to the problem?
    (a) Nehemiah 4:4

    (b) Nehemiah 4:15

❖ ❖ ❖
Make It Personal

Here are ten steps you can follow to help you solve your problems:

1. Never believe that any problem has *no* solution. Don't let anyone tell you "It can't be done." Nothing is impossible with God. Our God is a God of hope.

2. Clearly define the problem in writing (not just thinking). Writing it out helps you know exactly what the problem is, not just its symptoms. To help define it, ask, How would God define the problem?

3. Organize the problem and divide it into parts. Start working on the part that is easiest for you. When you get that done, start on another part. Soon you will see the problem shrink.

4. Find Scripture that applies to the problem. Ask yourself, What are the obstacles that stand in the way to keep me from solving the problem?

5. Specify some people that could help you. Identify some books and resources that could give you information. (Remember the Bible has the best information on problem solving.)

6. What are the possible actions you could take? Write them down.

7. Which of these actions could you try? Which one would God want you to try?

8. Decide which solution is best (the one most pleasing to God). Take action and do it.

9. Never let problems stop you from making the right decision even if the consequence is hard. God honors doing right.

10. Remember you cannot choose your problem, but you can choose your response. God did not make you a robot. He made you with a will and gave you the power to make a choice.

May God help us all make right choices!

❖ ❖ ❖
Put It into Practice
(For personal challenge, not class discussion.)

Rewrite here the problem that you wrote at the beginning of this lesson.

Apply the ten steps above to this problem. See if they help you solve the problem and help bring peace to your heart.

I trust these ten steps will be as great a blessing to you as they have been to me. Don't forget, we have a God who can do more than we ask or imagine (Ephesians 3:20). Trust Him to solve your problems—just like Nehemiah did!

LESSON 11

Rekindling Your Spiritual Passion
Nehemiah 1—13

NEHEMIAH is a challenge to busy people to be fully committed and obedient to God. The purpose of this study is to examine Nehemiah's zeal and passion to do the task God had put into his heart and to challenge us to have the same kind of zeal. Nehemiah's example leaves us without excuse for not serving God wholeheartedly. Nehemiah did what was seemingly impossible.

Life is full of challenges and confrontations; it is a series of problem-solving situations. Nehemiah had the keys that unlocked problems: (1) he knew how to communicate with God; (2) he knew how to respond to the king; (3) he knew how to motivate disheartened, greedy, and discouraged people. His passion for God also helped him respond to God's enemies and their frequent and varied attacks. Many people have dreams of what they will do someday for God; Nehemiah achieved his dreams.

We often think of Nehemiah as the man who rebuilt the walls of Jerusalem, but he also rebuilt the Jewish people. Nehemiah was an ordinary layman with an extraordinary life. At least five times in this record of his life, he faced impossible situations. Each time, he responded by turning to God in prayer.

Nehemiah came from obscurity and then faced difficulties,

setbacks, and unbelievable oppositions that only seemed to bring out the finest in him and that gave him a place of greatness in Jewish history. May the example of Nehemiah's burning passion and zeal for God challenge and motivate us to serve God with more joy and enthusiasm than we ever have before.

Questions to ask yourself: What motivations drive my life each day? What exciting thing makes me want to get out of bed each morning? What am I really fired up about?

God takes little and makes much out of it. He says if we have faith as a tiny grain of mustard seed, He can do great things for us. As you study this lesson, think about what tiny burning ember you have inside of you that you could allow God to turn into a roaring fire. How can you increase your passion for God?

1. When Nehemiah heard of the situation in Jerusalem, he wept, mourned, fasted, and prayed. What does this response reveal about his feelings for Jerusalem (Nehemiah 1:2–4)?

2. What was the main purpose of Nehemiah's prayer in Nehemiah 1:11?

God works on us from the inside out. All great works for God start by a tiny spark planted in our hearts and minds. The possibility of Nehemiah's going to Jerusalem to build the wall was highly unlikely. It was like a tiny spark.

3. (a) Who works in us (Philippians 2:13)?

    (b) How does He work?

When we allow God to work in our hearts, He can take a tiny spark and make it become a roaring fire. New Christians are a good example of this. How exciting to be around new Christians! They want to see their friends and relatives accept Christ just as they did. They have an overwhelming passion to work for God. They are all out for God.

4. What did Nehemiah do to fan the spark God put into his heart (Nehemiah 2:13–16)?

When God calls us to do a task, we often have to survey the work alone, depending only on God for wisdom. Nehemiah was not qualified to be a builder. (He did not have a contractor's license.) He was a cupbearer by trade, but God had put a fire in his heart to do a great work.

Someone has said that the only career advice you will ever need is to find a passion and follow it. Some of the Jews may have said, "Nehemiah has no business building this wall. He has no experience in construction. The only thing he has ever done is help the king eat his fancy food." But Nehemiah ignored the criticism. He had a burning passion from God to build the wall. What about you? What does God have for you to do? Whatever it is, get excited about it!

Some ladies go to seminars and become excited about doing a task for God, but then they have to take the next step; they have to take some action. If they don't take that step, they will not grow in their Christian lives; they will not be able to influence others as they should, and they will not allow God to do the great work in their lives that He wants to do. They need motivation to keep going.

5. (a) How did Nehemiah motivate the people, as recorded in Nehemiah 2:17?

(b) What motivation did he use in 2:18?

Wouldn't you like to have heard what Nehemiah said? No doubt he told the people how God had spoken to him when he was in Persia and had given him favor with the king. The people knew God's hand of blessing was on Nehemiah, and they shouted, "Let's build!"

6. Has God done some exciting things for you in the past? Do you have a story of God's blessing that you could share with the group? (Your story could be the encouragement someone else needs.) Summarize your story here.

When we are obedient to the fire God has put within us, it will spread to others. A fire never stays the same—either it spreads, or it dies out. So, how do we keep it burning? How do we preserve it? Perseverance and passion seem to go together.

7. What three qualities that pertain to perseverance and passion are mentioned in 1 Corinthians 15:58?

8. Galatians 6:9 teaches us that perseverance pays. What does this verse tell us *not* to do? Why?

9. First Corinthians 9:24-27 challenges us to have passion and perseverance.

(a) Verse 24 compares life to training for what sporting event?

(b) What must we do to be winners (vv. 25–27)?

10. How are we to do our life's work (Colossians 3:17)?

Passion causes you to enjoy the work of reaching your goal as much as enjoying the completed accomplishment. There is a real satisfaction in reaching your goal; but what you actually enjoy most is talking about your journey to get there.

11. Near the end of his life Paul reviewed the work God had entrusted him to do. What did he say about his life's journey in 2 Timothy 4:7?

How will you view your life when it is time to meet God?

People with a passion for God let God speak to them. Nehemiah heard of the problems in Jerusalem from his brother, Hanani, but God was the One Who put the spark in his heart to rebuild the walls. This happened as Nehemiah spent time with God (Nehemiah 1:4). We, too, need to spend time in solitude with God. Jesus set a good example of this for us.

12. What did Jesus do in the following verses?
    (a) Matthew 14:23

    (b) Mark 1:35

If Jesus needed a solitary place to meet with God, surely we do too.

Just as Nehemiah gave the people some admonitions in order to keep their passion for serving God alive and flourishing, we, too, need some admonitions.

13. What are we told to do in Ephesians 6:10 and 11?

Never take God's fire for granted and assume it will always be there, because it won't. Fire has a tendency to burn out; that is just its nature. I grew up in a big old farmhouse that had a wood-burning stove in the living room. As long as I stayed close to the stove, I was warm (at least on one side), but when I moved away from the stove, I became cold. To get warm again, I had to go back to the stove.

How is your service for God? Have you gotten away from the fire, or passion, of God? Do you need to go back to the "stove"?

14. Sometimes when we have gotten away from God's fire, we need to claim some of His promises to help us get back. What promise is found in Philippians 1:6?

In rekindling our spiritual passion, we need to incorporate three principles:

• **We need to know God's plan for our lives.** God reveals this plan to us as we spend time with Him in prayer and reading His Word.

• **We need strong convictions** to live our lives according to the plan He has revealed to us.

• **We need to believe that our God is greater than the problems we face.**

These three principles will help us live so that when we see Christ, He will say, "Well done, good and faithful servant."

❈ ❈ ❈
Make It Personal

According to the following verses, what can we expect from the future when we are obeying God's commands with great delight (passion)?

Psalm 112:1-3

Psalm 112:4-9

❈ ❈ ❈
Put It into Practice
(For personal challenge, not class discussion.)

A burning passion for God takes us beyond being average Christians. It causes us to do things that we normally would not do. It makes us different from those around us. It allows God to bless us because we have gone to a new level.

I experienced this when we moved to a new neighborhood. I felt a spark inside that kept saying, Why don't you have a neighborhood ladies' Bible study? I ignored the idea for a year, but the thought just kept coming into my mind. Finally I said, "Okay, Lord, I'll try it." But in my heart I wondered if anybody would want to come. Everyone was very busy. I was older than most of the ladies. But they did come! I'm glad that I listened to God and allowed Him to use me.

1. Summarize your answers to the questions at the beginning of this lesson.

2. Did a thought or a Scripture verse in this lesson stand out to you because you know it could apply to your answer above? If yes, write it here.

3. Imagine you were at your own funeral. What could people say about you? What would you like them to be able to say about you? What changes would you need to make in your life for them to say this?

4. What steps can you take immediately to incorporate this change into your life?

LESSON 12

Lessons from Nehemiah

WE HAVE spent the last eleven lessons studying a person named Nehemiah. He is not mentioned anywhere in the Bible except in the book that bears his name. God chose this man to teach us how to face life's problems.

(1) Nehemiah prayed short prayers in the middle of crisis situations.

(2) He was willing to sacrifice the pleasures of the palace to do God's work in primitive living conditions.

(3) He tackled a seemingly impossible task by praying and depending on God to answer his prayers and to work out his problems.

(4) He was a leader of people, a great organizer, and a master motivator. He took a group of discouraged Jews who were living in ruins and motivated them to "rise up and build" the wall around Jerusalem.

(5) He was not shaken when Sanballat and Tobiah made fun of his hard work. He realized that the men were troublemakers, and he "considered the source." No matter how discouraging the situation became, he just kept on building—doing the job God wanted him to do. He looked to God to reward him for doing right. He did not become sidetracked.

(6) He stirred the people to return to God's house, he turned their hearts toward the worship of God, and he reinstated the Feast of Tabernacles.

(7) He feared God more than he feared man.

(8) He was a deeply spiritual yet exceptionally practical

man. Both spirituality and practicality are taught in Scripture. Nehemiah had the right combination of both.

Questions to ask yourself: What lessons does God want to teach me from Nehemiah? How can I incorporate these lessons into my daily life?

1. Why were we given the biographies of great people in the Old Testament? Read 1 Corinthians 10:11.

2. Quickly scan Nehemiah 1. How did Nehemiah show concern for God's work?

3. Nehemiah's prayer in chapter 1 has several principles that we can apply to our prayers today. What are these principles?

We know that God was pleased with Nehemiah's prayer because He granted his request. He changed the heart of a Gentile king.

4. Read Nehemiah 2:1-5. Identify at least two principles for handling fear.

5. (a) Apparently Nehemiah had been doing some planning as well as praying. When the king asked, "What do you want?" (Nehemiah 2:4), how did Nehemiah answer that question (v. 5)?

(b) For what did he ask the king (vv. 7–9)?

Not much is said about the 800-mile trip to Jerusalem, but Nehemiah did not exactly find a welcoming party when he arrived. Sanballat and Tobiah were quite upset that someone had come to help the Jews (Nehemiah 2:10).

6. What are some things Nehemiah did in order to motivate the people to build the wall (Nehemiah 2:11–18)?

7. What are some lessons we can learn from Nehemiah on how to motivate people in our lives?

Once Nehemiah had the people convinced to build, you would think his problems would be over, wouldn't you? But problems are never over as long as we are on this earth.

8. Look at the next problem that arose (Nehemiah 2:19) and note how Nehemiah responded to it (v. 20). What lesson for life can we learn from it?

Chapter 3 is a registry of names. Nehemiah recognized the people for their work. He placed them to work near their homes or special places of interest. He focused on his work and did not

104 FACING LIFE'S PROBLEMS

become sidetracked when the nobles refused to work.

Chapter 4 could be titled "Pray and Fight the Enemy." Nehemiah had no difficulty combining the spiritual and the military.

9. What tactics did Sanballat and Tobiah use to hinder God's workers (Nehemiah 4:1-3, 7, 8)?

10. What two things did Nehemiah do to oppose the enemy (Nehemiah 4:9)?

11. Everyone is criticized at one time or other. Sometimes we are put down for things we can control; at other times we are lambasted for things beyond our control. Name some ways of handling criticism that would be pleasing to God.

12. Nehemiah 5 teaches us some lessons in the area of finance. What does it tell us about the following subjects? (The verses in Proverbs will help stimulate your thinking on this subject.)
   (a) Taking advantage of the poor (Nehemiah 5:7; Proverbs 21:13; 22:16)

   (b) Greed (Nehemiah 5:8; Proverbs 15:27; 23:4, 5)

(c) Helping the poor (Nehemiah 5:8, 10, 11; Proverbs 22:9; 28:27; 31:20)

(d) Honesty (Nehemiah 5:13; Proverbs 16:8, 11)

In chapter 6 we see that Sanballat, Tobiah, Geshem, and the rest of the Jews' enemies had not given up. First they had tried to sidetrack Nehemiah to get him to the plain of Ono, but he said, "O no!" Then they accused him of appointing prophets and making himself king. He prayed another short prayer. They still did not give up. The next time, they tried to trick him into going into the temple so he wouldn't be killed. Nehemiah saw through their scheme, stuck to his work, and accomplished his goal.

Satan works hard to hinder our spiritual goals. If he cannot stop us one way, he will try another way. One of his best tools against the believer is discouragement.

13. (a) To keep from becoming discouraged, what are some things Nehemiah *did not* do in chapter 6?

(b) How can we apply his example to our lives?

Chapter 7 is a list of the exiles who returned to Jerusalem. Because their cultural identity was threatened, the Jews kept careful records of their ancestry.

In chapter 8 we see Nehemiah fade to the background as

Ezra rises to the front, leading in prayer and the reading of Scripture. The Jews stood and listened to Ezra read God's Word from daybreak until noon. They wept because they had disobeyed it. Nehemiah and Ezra urged the people to stop weeping. Sadness did not suit the sacred day. Ezra told them, "The joy of the LORD is your strength." Knowing what God's Word says changed their lives.

14. What are some ways God's Word can change your life . . .
    (a) as you read it (Revelation 1:3)?

    (b) as you meditate on it (Psalm 1:2, 3)?

    (c) as you memorize it (Psalm 119:11)?

In chapter 13 Nehemiah asked the question, "Why is the house of God forsaken?" (v. 11). After Nehemiah had returned to Babylon, the Jews returned to their ungodly ways. Tobiah (of all people) was allowed to live in the temple. Upon returning to Jerusalem, Nehemiah threw Tobiah out of the temple (then cleansed it), reinstated the temple services, and stopped the merchants from selling on the Sabbath.

15. "Why is the house of God forsaken?" is a good question to ask ourselves today. Answer the following questions about church attendance.
    (a) What can church attendance do for your spiritual life?

    (b) What can you do to make your church attendance more meaningful?

We see throughout the book of Nehemiah that Nehemiah faced many fearful situations: facing the king when Nehemiah was sad, asking the king for favors, and constantly dealing with the enemies of God who tried to intimidate him by creating fearful crises. Nehemiah did not let fear stop him.

16. What are some resources that God has given us to help us face our fears today?

Nehemiah had multitudes of problems, but he knew how to handle them.

17. How do you think God wants us to respond to our problems?

Nehemiah was noted for his spiritual passion and fire for God. How about you? How is your fire for God? Is there anyone who tries to put out your fire for God? If so, let's call that person a firefighter.

Watch out for firefighters! They look for fires and try to put them out. They use tactics like this:
- It won't work; we've tried it before.
- Why change? I like things the way they are.
- We've never done it that way before.
- I think this is a great idea, but it will work best somewhere else.

Firefighters have a questioning spirit aimed at discrediting your work for God. It is not wrong to ask questions, but I am referring to a questioning spirit with wrong motives. Nehemiah faced this in chapter 4, not just once but nine times.

Firefighters hinder people with great potential from going to the top. If God has called you to be a housewife and a mother, some people may view your calling as unimportant—perhaps even lazy. Regardless of your God-given task, you will encounter criticism sometimes.

Firefighters have one benefit: they make us look at our motives. They make us evaluate whether we truly have a mandate from God to do the task before us, or whether we are on some tangent.

Who are the firefighters in your life? They may not always be unsaved people; many times they are Christians or relatives.

Nehemiah stayed on course because he focused on what God wanted him to do.

18. Read Philippians 3:13 and 14. How did Paul view the job God had given him to do on earth?

To keep the blaze of passion for God glowing in our lives, we need to hang around "fire<u>light</u>ers" and stay away from fire<u>fight</u>ers.

❀ ❀ ❀

Make It Personal

Nehemiah was an ordinary, practical person whose memoirs explain the great success God gave him. He is an example for us to follow. Summarize how each of the following words or phrases describe Nehemiah's life:

1. Person of prayer

2. Person of integrity

3. Unselfish person

Lessons from Nehemiah

4. Not easily sidetracked

5. Motivator

6. Not fearful

7. Person of conviction

Put It into Practice
(For personal challenge, not class discussion.)

1. Reread the list above and think about what application of these qualities God wants you to make in your life. Write your answer here.

2. What one outstanding truth did you get from the study of Nehemiah?

3. How can you apply this truth to your life?

Leader's Guide

Suggestions for Leaders

The effectiveness of a group Bible study usually depends on two things: (1) the leader herself and (2) the ladies' commitment to prepare beforehand and interact during the study. You cannot totally control the second factor, but you have total control over the first one. These brief suggestions will help you be an effective Bible study leader.

You will want to prepare each lesson a week in advance. During the week, read supplemental material and look for illustrations in the everyday events of your life as well as in the lives of others.

Encourage the ladies in the Bible study to complete each lesson before the meeting itself. This preparation will make the discussion more interesting. You can suggest that ladies answer two or three questions a day as part of their daily Bible reading time rather than trying to do the entire lesson at one sitting.

The physical setting in which you meet will have some bearing on the study itself. An informal circle of chairs, chairs around a table, someone's living room or family room—these types of settings encourage people to relax and participate. In addition to an informal setting, create an atmosphere in which ladies feel free to participate and be themselves.

During the discussion time, here are a few things to observe:
• Don't do all the talking. This is not designed to be a lecture.
• Encourage discussion on each question by adding ideas and questions.
• Don't discuss controversial issues that will divide the group. (Differences of opinion are healthy; divisions are not.)
• Don't allow one lady to dominate the discussion. Use statements such as these to draw others into the study: "Let's hear from someone on this side of the room" (the side opposite the dominant talker); "Let's hear from someone who has not shared yet today."
• Stay on the subject. The tendency toward tangents is always possible in a discussion. One of your responsibilities as the leader is to keep the group on track.
• Don't get bogged down on a question that interests only one person.

You may want to use the last fifteen minutes of the scheduled time for prayer. If you have a large group of ladies, divide into smaller groups for prayer. You could call this the "Share and Care Time."

If you have a morning Bible study, encourage the ladies to go out for lunch with someone else from time to time. This is a good way to get acquainted with new ladies. Occasionally you could plan a time when ladies bring their own lunches or salads to share and eat together. These things help promote fellowship and friendship in the group.

The formats that follow are suggestions only. You can plan your own format, use one of these, or adapt one of these to your needs.

2-hour Bible Study
10:00—10:15	Coffee and fellowship time
10:15—10:30	Get-acquainted time
	Have two ladies take five minutes each to tell something about themselves and their families.
	Also use this time to make announcements and, if appropriate, take an offering for the babysitters.
10:30—11:45	Bible study
	Leader guides discussion of the questions in the day's lesson.
11:45—12:00	Prayer time

2-hour Bible Study
10:00—10:45	Bible lesson
	Leader teaches a lesson on the content of the material. No discussion during this time.
10:45—11:00	Coffee and fellowship
11:00—11:45	Discussion time
	Divide into small groups with an appointed leader for each group. Discuss the questions in the day's lesson.
11:45—12:00	Prayer time

1½-hour Bible Study
10:00—10:30	Bible study
	Leader guides discussion of half the questions in the day's lesson.
10:30—10:45	Coffee and fellowship
10:45—11:15	Bible study
	Leader continues discussion of the questions in the day's lesson.
11:15—11:30	Prayer time

Answers for Leader's Use

Information inside parentheses ( ) is additional instruction for the group leader.

Lesson 1
1. He wept, mourned, prayed, and fasted.
2. Harboring sin in our hearts hinders God's answering our prayers.
3. When the Holy Spirit points out sin to us, we should immediately confess it.
4. He spoke of the great and awesome ("terrible") God, Who keeps His word and shows mercy to those who love Him.
5. God curses the person who trusts in his own strength and who departs from the Lord. God blesses those who trust Him and depend on His strength.
6. He and his father's house.

114   FACING LIFE'S PROBLEMS

7. Forgive them because God forgave us.
8. (a) He acknowledged his sins to God; he had them on his mind at all times. (b) Against God.
9. He called it a sin against God (even though it was also a sin against Potiphar and his wife [Exodus 20:14] and even Joseph himself [1 Corinthians 6:18]).
10. To come to God in prayer boldly (with confidence) to receive mercy and grace to help in time of need.
11. Remember.
12. *(Divide into four groups. Ask each group to look up a verse and give an answer.)* John 14:13, 14—God will answer the "whatsoever" needs of our lives. Hebrews 11:6—God rewards those who come to Him in faith. 1 John 5:14, 15—We can approach God with confidence when we pray according to His will, knowing He hears and will answer. Jeremiah 33:3—God's answers to prayer are greater than our fondest imaginations.
13. Keep a journal of prayer requests and answers; tell children and friends about answers to prayer; keep mementos that remind you of God's answers; give public testimony to God's answers.
14. To give him success by granting him mercy (favor) with the king.
15. (a) Three loaves of bread. (b) He persisted in his request. (c) Be persistent in prayer by asking, seeking and knocking.

Make It Personal:

A time to pray—It helps to develop the habit of praying. It keeps us consistent in our prayer life. A plan to pray—It is a reminder of things we need to pray about. A journal of answered prayer—It helps us know when our prayers are answered; it increases our faith. When we see what God has done for us in the past, it gives us hope (faith) that He will help us with the future. Difficult situations—They remind us that we must turn to God in faith. Our problems are too big to solve ourselves; only God can solve them.

Lesson 2

1. He asked the king for permission to go (v. 5), protection to get there (v. 7), and materials to build the wall (v. 8).
2. A direct answer to Nehemiah's prayer. The king would never have asked the question without Nehemiah's prayer.
3. The king granted his request.
4. God controls kings, so Nehemiah's first action was not to go to the king, but to God.
5. It shows us that doing things God's way pays. Even when it seems like a bad choice at first, eventually we will see that God's way is best (Isaiah 55:9).
6. He knew God was great and kept his Word to those who love and obey Him. He viewed God as One to reverence and as One Who could grant his petitions.

Leader's Guide 115

7. Jeremiah 32:17, 27—Nothing is too hard for God. Luke 1:37; 18:27—Nothing is impossible with God.
8. They remind us that nothing is too hard for God. With God, no problem is impossible to solve. *(The ladies may share other ideas.)*
9. A person's face reflects the feelings of her heart. Problems and concerns that cause heartache are reflected in a person's face and attitude.
10. (a) He was afraid. (b) Nehemiah was risking his life. If the king were offended, Nehemiah would be killed.
11. He trusted in the Lord, realizing that God controlled the length of his life.
12. Can I help you? He wanted Nehemiah to tell him how to help.
13. If we pray to God in times of trouble, He will deliver us and honor us.
14. The work in Jerusalem was to be stopped and not started again unless decreed by the king.
15. (a) How long will it take to build the walls? When will you come back? (b) He didn't want to lose Nehemiah permanently; he was eager to have him return.
16. It can help us realize that none of our problems are impossible. Seeing how God answered Nehemiah's prayers increases our faith to believe He will answer our prayers. We are not to fear man, but trust God to do the impossible for us.

Make It Personal:
(1) He loved God because He hears and answers prayer. The psalmist would pray during his whole life. (2) We see how God heard and answered Nehemiah's prayers. Nehemiah's prayers are recorded throughout the book of Nehemiah, and Nehemiah lived for God. (3) Since we know God hears and answers our prayers, we should love God and pray as long as we live. We should trust Him for the impossible. We should trust Him for every need in our lives, whether great or small.

Lesson 3
1. (a) He needed them to help him build the wall. One man could not accomplish the job alone. (b) Because they are valuable to God. Christ died for all people. We are responsible to influence them to accept Christ as Savior. Not one of us is an island; we need others to encourage us and help us as we serve the Lord.
2. *(A Bible study leader should never put people on the spot in a group. Prior to the class session, ask someone to share a brief testimony of how she received Christ.)*
3. Sanballat the Horonite and Tobiah the Ammonite.
4. He felt they were important.
5. Nehemiah came to help the Jews—not to prosper himself. *(See also Nehemiah 5:14–16.)*
6. He reminded them of the plight of Jerusalem and the disgrace they

116 FACING LIFE'S PROBLEMS

were to the surrounding nations. Then he told them how God had blessed him and had made his trip possible. The people responded, "Let's build."
7. When God calls us to do a task, He will also enable us to do it.
8. Take interest in their interests; listen to them; treat them with honor and respect; compliment them; recognize their achievements.
9. (a) By giving him material gifts and refreshing his spirit. (b) He believed that those men deserved to be recognized.
10. (a) Nehemiah 2:17, 20a—geese. Nehemiah encouraged the people to do a great work for God. Nehemiah 2:10, 19—chickens. Sanballat, Tobiah, and Geshem mocked and ridiculed the Jews, hoping to discourage them from building the wall. (b) Pray for them and their needs; take an interest in them; encourage them to get involved in things that would promote spiritual growth; share spiritual books and tapes that have been a blessing to you; remind them of God's faithfulness.
11. That God had put it into his heart to build the wall around Jerusalem.
12. Priests.
13. Nehemiah 3:10, "against his house"; v. 23, "against their house"; v. 28, "against the house"; v. 29, "against his house"; v. 30, "against his chamber."
14. Manipulation is management of a person, circumstances, or something else to one's own advantage. It is usually unfair and unscrupulous. Motivation, on the other hand, is the supply of a motive to cause a person to act in a particular way. It is not for one's own advantage, nor is it unfair or unscrupulous.
15. The wall was for their protection from the enemy, and it helped them retain their Jewish culture and language.
16. It helps you to do a job well. You can't work successfully if you don't know what is expected of you.
17. Near the sheep gate, possibly where the sheep used for sacrifice were herded into the city.
18. The phrase is "another piece" or "the other piece." They each did extra work.
19. (a) The nobles of the Tekoites. (b) Don't focus on troublemakers; ignore them if possible. Focus on the job God wants us to do. (c) He would not have been able to get the wall built in only fifty-two days.

Lesson 4
1. (a) He was angry and mocked them. He ridiculed the Jews in the presence of his associates. (b) They were feeble.
2. It would be of poor quality.
3. Noah obeyed and built an ark on dry ground, even though his peers probably made fun of him. He chose to believe God and not be swayed by the ridicule or doubts or rebellion of man.
4. (a) A fox could break it down. (b) It was flimsy, shoddy.

5. The things of the world do not last; doing what God wants us to do lasts eternally.
6. (a) He thought he could get more wealth and retire in luxury. He forgot that he would die and have to give an account of his life to God. (b) Pleasing God instead of himself; being thankful and generous to God.
7. (a) Sanballat the Horonite. (b) Tobiah the Ammonite. (c) Geshem the Arabian.
8. They reveal things such as honesty, integrity, spiritual interest, gossip (whether we do or don't). *(Have the ladies add to this list.)*
9. The enemies were angry because the Jews had succeeded in building the wall. They conspired to gather an army to fight Nehemiah and the Jews.
10. (a) They laughed at Him. (b) They mocked, ridiculed, and sneered at Him.
11. (a) Revile, or insult, us. (b) Persecute us. (c) Falsely accuse us of all kinds of evil.
12. We will be rewarded in Heaven.
13. (a) Being ridiculed (suffering) for doing right. *(Ask a volunteer to give an example of being ridiculed for doing right, but being blessed by God for doing right anyway.)* (b) Sanctify (or set apart) Christ as Lord. (c) Give an answer to anyone who asks what Christ has done for us ("a reason of the hope" in us, v. 15). (d) With meekness (gentleness) and fear (reverence). (e) Giving out tracts, inviting people to church, telling them what a difference Christ has made in our lives. *(Have the ladies add to the list.)* (f) The way you respond by keeping a clear conscience and good behavior.
14. (a) Good. (b) We are expected to suffer for wrongdoing. Suffering for doing right with a good attitude is a wonderful testimony of Christ living through us.
15. The Jews' enemies were afraid and lost their self-confidence because they realized that God had helped the Jews.
16. Christ will be exalted; everyone will bow to Him and confess Him as Lord.
17. Don't seek revenge for the wrongs that someone has done to you.
18. The people had a mind to work.
19. Live in peace with others. Do not repay evil for evil, but be kind and loving to those (even family members) who ridicule us.

Lesson 5
1. It means we have accepted Christ as our personal Savior. We realized we were sinners, we believed Christ died for our sins, and we trusted Him to be our Savior. *(Explain the plan of salvation more fully if you have unsaved ladies in the class.)*
2. (a) The people of Judah. (b) There was so much rubbish that they became weary of clearing it all.

3. Moses, David, Elijah. *(Ask the ladies to add to the list.)*
4. (a) Overwork, stressful relationships, things we can't control, people telling us we cannot do something. *(Add to the list.)* (b) Eat, don't eat, talk, don't talk, spend money, withdraw from people, quit, cry on someone else's shoulder, become depressed. Some do what they should; they turn to God for help.
5. Half of its height.
6. Schedule a night out together. Set aside some time to talk every day (when you get home from work; before you go to sleep, etc.). Share the same interests. Try to get away for a couple of days occasionally. Pray together. Go to church together. *(Encourage the ladies to share.)*
7. Attack and kill them.
8. If the people depended on their own strength, they would fail. They needed God's strength.
9. With wisdom, understanding, and knowledge.
10. Things that are true, honest (noble), just (right), pure, lovely, of good report (admirable).
11. We become what we think.
12. Have faith in God. Faith can move mountains. If you pray with faith, you will receive.
13. He armed them and posted guards to watch for the enemy. He reminded them that they could fight for their families and that God is greater than the enemy.
14. They teach lessons of life and give us hope and encouragement.
15. When he fails, he will get up and try again. Discouraging circumstances do not cause him to quit.
16. (a) It tells us not to worry about our daily needs, because God knows what they are and will provide for us. (b) People who don't know God worry about certain things, but since we do know God, we should be concerned about seeking God's kingdom and righteousness. He knows our needs and will provide for them; we should trust Him.
17. (a) If the people heard a trumpet, they were to gather wherever the trumpet had been sounded from. (b) God would fight their battle. (c) God.

Lesson 6
1. (a) The people did not have enough to eat. (b) They were mortgaging their lands and vineyards, but they were probably going to lose them. (c) They were borrowing money to pay taxes.
2. He was very angry.
3. (a) Taxing or charging interest to their own people (the Jews). (b) They were not to charge interest to their own people, especially the poor. (c) If their fellow countryman became poor and could not support himself, they were to help him ("relieve" him) so that he could continue to live among them. (d) charge "usury," or interest; sell food for profit; make a fellow Israelite work as a slave.

4. (a) He did not eat the food allotted to governors. (b) He did not buy their land from them. (c) He feared and reverenced God.
5. (a) On earth. (b) In Heaven. (c) Because they cannot be destroyed or stolen; they are secure in Heaven. (d) Sparingly and bountifully, or abundantly. (e) We are not to give grudgingly (reluctantly) or feeling that we "have" to give, but we are to give cheerfully. (f) They will have what they need and will abound in every good work.
6. (a) Proverbs 11:24—You get more by giving than by not giving. Proverbs 11:25—Generosity brings prosperity; when you help others, you help yourself. Proverbs 11:26—People curse the stingy, but blessings come to those who are willing to part with their possessions. (b) If you give to God, in return He will give to you abundantly. (c) Personal answers, which could include things such as a nice home, beautiful clothes, and adequate money. (d) Appetite, eternal life, friends, good home life, happiness, health, knowledge, loving companionship, peace, purpose to live, sleep.
7. They cannot take their things with them to Heaven; things are only earthly.
8. (a) They are not to be proud of wealth or put hope in it, because it is uncertain; but they are to hope in the Lord, Who provides things for our enjoyment. (b) Riches do not last and are exceedingly uncertain.
9. We cannot serve both God and material things; we cannot have two masters.
10. (a) God gives the power to get wealth; He gives us our possessions. (b) We should praise and thank Him.
11. (a) If a person doesn't work, he shouldn't eat either. (b) A lazy person does not take care of his possessions. The writer looked at a lazy man's field and vineyard; thorns and weeds had grown everywhere. When he analyzed why the land was like that, he realized that the brambles were a result of laziness. Laziness will cause poverty to overtake us as well.
12. (a) If we trust in riches, we will fail; but if we trust in righteousness, we will flourish. (b) We cannot take our material wealth to Heaven.
13. Wanting to get rich (love of money) can cause us to fall into temptation and sin. Note: The "love of money," not "money," is the cause of sin.

Lesson 7
1. They had an assembly and asked Ezra to bring out the Scriptures. He read to them from daybreak until noon.
2. (a) Converts (revives) the soul. (b) Makes the simple wise. (c) Give joy to the heart. (d) Give light to the eyes (understanding). (e) Show us what is true and righteous.
3. Gold and honey.
4. (a) The Law. (b) For five or six hours. (c) Attentively. (d) To listen carefully; to think about what is being said. (e) We can try to

understand as much as possible as we hear it taught. We can ask the Holy Spirit to show us how God's Word applies to our lives.
5. (a) They said "amen," lifted up their hands, bowed their heads, and worshiped God with their faces to the ground. (b) They reverenced Him and worshiped Him. (c) When we start praising God for all He is and all He has done, we will automatically start worshiping too.
6. The Levites' job was to instruct the people so that they could understand God's Word.
7. By formally teaching them from the Bible, living the Christian life, and being an example. By the way we talk, our attitude toward life and God, our business transactions, by being honest *(Ask the ladies to mention as many ways as possible.)*
8. They heard the words of the Law and realized they had not obeyed them.
9. A broken and contrite heart
10. "The joy of the LORD is your strength."
11. We are to have His joy in us. Our joy is to be complete (or full).
12. (a) They built booths as they were told. (b) Since the days of Joshua. (c) They celebrated as they were told and had an assembly on the eighth day.
13. (a) Teach it to their children; talk about it in all situations and at various times in the day; bind it on their hands and between their eyes; write it on their houses. (b) We can use every opportunity of family life to talk about and apply God's Word; we can put Scripture verses in places where we can see them, such as on the refrigerator or above the kitchen sink or on the bathroom mirror or in a visible place in the car; we can carry a verse in our purses or pockets; we can decorate our homes with Scripture plaques. *(Ask the ladies to give other suggestions.)*

Make It Personal:
(1) For doctrine, reproof, correction, instruction in righteousness. (2) *(Ask the ladies for ideas for good Bible reading plans.)* (3) a—Not just listen to the Word; b—obey it; do what it says. (4) So that he would not sin against God. (5) Meditate on it; think about it. *(Ask the ladies to share when they review Scripture passages they have learned.)*

Lesson 8
1. They intermarried with the heathen. Their children could not speak the Jewish language or understand the Jewish Scriptures.
2. (a) Verse 14 commands us not to have a yoke, or a bond, with an unbeliever. Marriage is a yoke; therefore, a believer and unbeliever should not marry. Both verses ask rhetorical questions to point out that believers and unbelievers don't belong together. (b) The media and our children's peers hold few of God's standards. Both subtly and overtly they teach that we should do whatever pleases us at the time. They claim we can do whatever we want, with no regard to God's law.

3. Listen to the Word of God (hear it) and obey (keep) it.
4. By hearing God's Word.
5. To devote himself to reading the Bible, hearing it explained (preaching), and doctrine (Biblical teaching).
6. (a) They were working and buying and selling. (b) Not to buy or sell on the Sabbath Day and to keep it holy; to honor the Sabbath year by not working the land in the seventh year; to cancel debts.
7. Businesses are open on Sunday; some people choose to work on Sunday because they get paid more for weekend work; people work so hard all week (including on Saturday) they are too tired to go to church on Sunday, or they want to use that day to do the things they couldn't get done during the week. *(Ask the ladies for other ideas.)*
8. It was a sign between God and the Israelites to remind them of their relationship to Him.
9. God would burn Jerusalem with unquenchable fire (destroy it).
10. We may gain material wealth, but we could lose our love for God and perhaps our families. When we stand before God, we will regret having put material things first.
11. Stayed outside the gates of Jerusalem once or twice.
12. The Levites had not been given their wages, so they left God's work to support themselves by farming.
13. To start tithing again.
14. It commands believers to bring their tithes when they attend church.
15. There would be an abundance of money to do God's work.
16. *(Ask for a volunteer to give a testimony about how God has blessed her for giving to Him.)*
17. Gave him a chamber (room) in the temple.
18. That if the people kept doing them and did not listen to and honor God, He would send a curse on them.
19. He asked God to remember what he had done (apparently right things).

Make It Personal:
(1) By showing love for God's house, attending regularly, letting the children know it is a priority in their parents' life. *(Note a negative influence is also possible. Have the ladies discuss this question.)* (2) Physically: getting clothes ready, getting a good night of sleep so we can feel well when we go to church, getting ready early enough so that we do not become frustrated before we get to church, having an adequate breakfast *(Add to this list.)* Spiritually: praying for the pastor's message to speak to our hearts, preparing our hearts and minds before we get to church. *(Add to this list.)* (3) When you attend church regularly, you convey the importance of church attendance in your life.

Lesson 9
1. The people's unbelief.

2. He has not given the spirit of fear; He has gives the spirit of power, love, and a sound (disciplined) mind.
3. Nehemiah 6:1, 2, 4—Nehemiah's enemies wanted to meet with him; 6:3—He said he was too busy to leave his work. Nehemiah 6:5–7—The enemies accused Nehemiah of leading the people to rebel; 6:8—Nehemiah said that what they had said was untrue; they made up the accusations. Nehemiah 6:10—The enemies tried to get Nehemiah to meet them in the temple to save his life; 6:11, 12—Nehemiah said he had no need to flee; he realized this was a setup.
4. He rebuked them for selling on the Sabbath and reminded them that God had judged their ancestors for doing the very same thing.
5. (a) To forget the past and to focus on the future. (b) These verses help us not to focus on past failures but to believe that God will help us in the future. They help us move on.
6. He supervised a major building project even though he wasn't a builder; he stood up to the enemies; he confronted his own people when necessary.
7. (a) It is a snare, a trap. (b) Trusting in God gives us safety.
8. It assures us that Jesus is always the same; He never changes.
9. Pray about the matter; thank God for all He does for us; appropriate His peace. *(Someone may be willing to relate a personal experience when the Philippians 4:6 and 7 formula has helped her with anxiety.)*
10. What wicked people fear will eventually happen; but if we live right, our desires will be granted.
11. Nehemiah trusted God when he went before the king; when he rallied the people to "arise and build"; when he did not take his rightful allotment as governor; when he reestablished the observance of the Sabbath. Nehemiah also trusted God to provide the funds and provisions for him to go to Jerusalem, to protect him from Sanballat and Tobiah, and to provide for him materially.
12. God orders, or controls, our lives.
13. We are to trust God, not our own understanding; God has promised to guide us.
14. He prayed, and God delivered him from his fears.
15. A vapor that vanishes.
16. God is with us.
17. (a) We need to number our days, or make them count. (b) We need God's mercy to live happy, joyful lives. (c) We need to have God establish our work, to bless it.
18. We should control our thoughts by tearing down the destructive ones and thinking only thoughts that God wants us to think.

Lesson 10

1. Nehemiah 1:3, 4—problem: Nehemiah received word concerning the state of affairs in Jerusalem; reaction: he wept, mourned, fasted, and prayed. 2:1, 2, 4—problem: The king noticed Nehemiah's sad face;

Leader's Guide 123

reaction: Nehemiah prayed. 4:1-6—problem: Sanballat and Tobiah tried to hinder the work with threats and mocking; reaction: Nehemiah prayed and continued to build. 6:1-9—problem: The enemies tried to get Nehemiah to leave the work and meet with them; reaction: Nehemiah refused to be persuaded by their threats and lies.
2. Jerusalem lay in waste, and its gates were burned with fire.
3. He appealed to their pride and challenged them *not* to be a disgrace, but to build. Then he told them the accounts of how God had changed the king's heart and how he had given Nehemiah provisions to rebuild the wall.
4. To set our minds on heavenly things.
5. To pursue our God-given goals persistently; to plan ahead.
6. (a) We should be humble, allowing God to bring honor if He so desires. (b) Give them to Jesus, because He cares for us. (c) He wants to devour and defeat us. (d) Be on guard against him, resist him, and stand firm in our faith in God.
7. (a) We can pray to God in trouble, and He will deliver us. He gives us long life. (b) Remembering God's commands and doing them gives a person long life and prosperity. (c) Wisdom, which comes from fearing God, protects and adds to our life. (d) Honoring our parents helps us live long.
8. People who love to just lie around and sleep all the time will probably be poor. People who love pleasure will be poor.
9. He prayed to God for help and just kept on doing his God-given task.
10. Moses chose to be identified with God's people (which involved living a life pleasing to God) rather than enjoy the pleasures of sin for a short time.
11. (a) Come to Him. (b) He will give us rest. (c) Take His yoke and learn of Him. (d) He will give rest to our souls.
12. (a) He prayed. (b) He returned to work.

Lesson 11
1. It shows his deep concern and his passion for his native country.
2. To ask God to work in the heart of the king so that he would allow Nehemiah to rebuild the wall of Jerusalem.
3. (a) God. (b) According to His good will and pleasure (as He desires to work in us).
4. He surveyed the situation so that he could organize the job.
5. (a) He reminded them of the ruins and devastation of Jerusalem and how bad that made them look ("a reproach"). (b) He told them the wonderful story of how God had caused the king to allow him to go to Jerusalem to build the wall.
6. *(Encourage one or two volunteers to tell how God undertook for them in a specific situation.)*
7. Steadfastness; unmovable; "abounding" in (giving yourself fully to) the work of God.

8. Don't be weary in doing good, because you will reap a good harvest if you don't give up.
9. (a) A race. (b) Train for the race. Discipline our lives.
10. We are to do it in the name of the Lord, giving thanks to Him.
11. He said that he had fought a fight for God and had finished what God had called him to do. He had kept the faith.
12. (a) He went alone on a mountainside to pray. (b) He went before daybreak to a solitary place to pray.
13. Be strong in the Lord. Put on the full armor of God so that we can stand against the Devil.
14. The God Who started a good work in us will complete it.

Make It Personal:
   Psalm 112:1-3—To be blessed; to have mighty and blessed children; to have wealth and riches; to be righteous. 112:4-9—Light in darkness; good to come to us; not to be shaken; to be remembered; to have no fear of bad news; to be steadfast; to trust in the Lord; to be secure; to be honored.

Lesson 12
1. They are examples for us to follow the good and to avoid the bad.
2. He asked about it (v. 2); he wept, fasted, mourned, and prayed (v. 4).
3. Possible answers are to worship God by acknowledging his greatness (v. 5); to confess our sins and those of our countrymen (vv. 6, 7); to claim God's past promises (vv. 8, 9); to ask that God grant our request (v. 11).
4. Speak up anyway. Even though Nehemiah was frightened, he spoke up and asked the king about the burden on his heart. Pray. Nehemiah prayed, trusting God to answer his prayer. He believed God controlled the hearts of men to accomplish His purpose. *(See if the ladies can add any other principles.)*
5. (a) He asked to rebuild the city of his fathers (Jerusalem). Since the king had earlier ordered the building in Jerusalem to stop, using the words "city of my fathers" may have been more diplomatic than using the word "Jerusalem." (b) He asked for letters to give him safety on his trip. He asked for the keeper of the king's forest to give him lumber. (The king sent an army and horsemen with him—something he needed but had not asked for. This circumstance reminds us of Ephesians 3:20.)
6. Some possible answers are these: He waited three days. (Perhaps he prayed and did more planning.) Then he went out at night and surveyed the ruins of Jerusalem. He assembled the people, reminded them of the awful condition of Jerusalem, and challenged them to build so that they would not be a reproach. He then told them how God had blessed him and brought him to Jerusalem.
7. Possible answers include: Be patient. (Nehemiah waited three days before he did anything.) Be prepared with a plan for what you want

Leader's Guide 125

to accomplish. Challenge people with what will meet their needs. (Living conditions in Jerusalem were bad for the Jews—a wall would help—and they would no longer be a reproach. No one wants to be a reproach.) Share with people how God has been working in our lives.

8. Don't get sidetracked from your goal. When you attempt something, you can expect criticism. Trust the God of Heaven to prosper you amid criticism. Remember, nothing is impossible with God.
9. Ridicule, conspiracy, insults, threatening a military attack.
10. Prayed and posted a guard.
11. Some possible answers are these: Ignore it; consider the source; pray for God to give you strength to handle it; explain to the person who is criticizing why you did what you did. (This works sometimes; at other times it only makes matters worse.)
12. (a) If we do not help those in need, we cannot expect God to help us. Nehemiah helped the oppressed, and in return God helped him. Be generous. (b) Greed is the source of many financial problems. Greed caused the money problems in Nehemiah 5. Don't make having riches your primary goal in life, because they will neither last long nor satisfy your heart's desires. (c) God blesses generosity and giving to the poor. Nehemiah helped the poor who were oppressed by the rich. (d) Righteousness is better than gaining wealth. We should be honest in our financial dealings.
13. (a) Some possible answers are these: He did not let the enemy sidetrack him (vv. 3, 4). He did not let the enemy intimidate him (vv. 6–9). He did not let them frighten him into stopping work (vv. 10–13). He did not forget to pray for strength (v. 9). *(Add to these answers if possible.)* (b) *(Ask the ladies for ways to apply the answers above to life's problems in general. This should stimulate the ladies' thinking on how to apply the principles to their personal problems.)*
14. (a) God promises to bless those who read His Word. His Word tells us what to do. It is His love letter to us. (b) It brings stability and spiritual growth to your life (c) It will keep you from sin.
15. *(Encourage the ladies to discuss these questions and add to the answers.)* Possible answers include: it will (a) instruct and enrich you; you can learn from other believers; you will be encouraged as people are saved. (b) Go with a prayerful spirit; take notes on the sermon and discuss it with your family or friends; use your sermon notes in your daily devotions. *(Other answers are possible.)*
16. Prayer; promises of the Word of God; faith in God; the Holy Spirit's ministry. *(Ask the ladies to name other things that God has provided to help us deal with fear.)*
17. God wants us to bring our problems to Him (1 Peter 5:7) and by faith believe that He will take care of them for us.
18. He forgot the past (successes and failures) and pressed on toward his God-given goal.